FEARLESS

*Leadership Lessons
at the Crossroads*

STEVE JOHNS

GriffMor
PUBLISHING
CARMEL, IN

Published by
GriffMor Publishing | Carmel, IN

GriffMor
PUBLISHING

Publisher's Cataloging-in-Publication Data
Johns, Steve.

Fearless : leadership lessons at the crossroads / Steve Johns. – Carmel, IN : GriffMor Pub., 2023.

p. ; cm.

ISBN13: 978-0-9601161-0-2 (print HC)
978-0-9601161-1-9 (print SC)

1. Leadership—Case studies. 2. Crisis management—Case studies.
3. Covid-19 Pandemic, 2020—Influence—Case studies. I. Title.

HD57.7.J64 2023
658.4092—dc23

Executive editor: Paul Scade
Editorial review and proofread: Diana Morris
Interior image design: Brian Holl
Cover design: Eric Tufford
Interior design: Brooke Camfield
Project coordination: Dawn Lego, Kelly Velasquez-Hague, and Karrie Wozniak
Project collaboration and print coordination: Jenkins Group Inc. | www.jenkinsgroupinc.com

Printed in the United States of America
27   26   25   24   23   •   5   4   3   2   1

PRAISE AND PASSAGE

There are many books on leadership, but Fearless: Leadership Lessons at the Crossroads *is special. Rooted in stoic thinking and planted firmly in human-centered leadership, the book's powerful stories will make you think and inspire you to change your perspectives. Steve has navigated his company through the roughest of times with honesty and a sense of pride and perseverance that we should all aspire to.*

—**Mark Lacek, Co-Founder, OneCause (formerly BidPal)**

The updates were vital for maintaining a positive attitude and staying focused on adapting to the ever-changing situation. We needed Steve's reminder to think about our customers and be mindful of the challenges they were facing. Steve was super helpful keeping us on mission to increase customer fundraising. What really helped was that Steve reminded us of our values. He did this over several weeks, and it inspired me to go the extra mile for our customers and share this message with the team. Our values were our North Star to help us overcome incredible challenges.

—**James Rischar (proudly, OneCause)**

I would always look forward to Steve's very human and personal emails each week. At a time of utter confusion, disconnect, and isolation, they somehow brought clarity, connection, and togetherness to the team . . . a sense of "we got this!" As a music fan myself, I loved the song references he often would include as well!

—**Diana Fragnito (proudly, OneCause)**

Every company faces crossroads, but it's the outcome and being undaunted in the face of adversity that matter most. Fearless *is full of important insights on how to lead and positively affect change in the midst of uncertainty.*

—**Don Aquilano, Co-Founder & Managing Director, Allos Ventures**

I have had the privilege of working with Steve four different times during our careers. During these challenging times, it is great to see him sharing decades of wisdom accumulated from a successful career in many different environments. There are lessons in these letters that can help people find a path to both professional and personal success. I recommend reading this book. It is a great illustration of relentless positive action!

—**Rick Snyder, former Governor of Michigan**

Steve Johns is one of those rare people who is both incredibly smart and deeply caring. In this day and age of bull$#!% and self-promotion, it's so refreshing to see a message of humility and truth as being the keys to real sustainable leadership. The easy way out is to lie and pretend but having the guts to really tell the truth is what truly makes a great leader. His lessons prove that a little honesty goes a long, long way, and to be humble and truthful is truly 'Fearless.'

—**Ted Waitt, Co-Founder, Gateway; Founder, Waitt Foundation and Waitt Institute**

Steve's updates reminded me what a nimble team I work with. We're all students, teachers, and sharers of knowledge, and the weekly emails really captured that spirit. Steve was busy sharing what he had learned with us, and at the same time he was learning himself and encouraging us to share back. I also loved that he shared the imperfection of his own life with us: he meditates to help handle the stress, he's working from a kitchen table . . . he was there with us. It made me feel that I didn't have to measure myself against something impossible. Both of my kids know Steve's name now because I'd call them over and read things out loud to them from the updates. They tease me about it now, but I've seen some of those ideas stick!

—Diane Dellafiora (proudly, OneCause)

A lot of the commentary in the business market was that, in this kind of crisis, you need a leader to take a command and control position. Like it's a war, right? So you need a Commander! And they have to grab the reins, give orders, and tell people what to do every step of the way. Yet that was not what Steve did. Instead, he inspired, he connected, he understood. He brought some real emotion to what he wrote, and I think that hit a lot of us in a different way to what we expected. He was going for inspiration rather than commands. And we really needed that in some of those tough weeks. As a result, everyone was able to rise to the occasion in special and unpredictable ways.

—Parrish Snyder (proudly, OneCause)

Fearless *is a moving account of the connection between a Chief Executive Officer, his team, and their customers—and how humanity comes forward in trying times. Bursting with practical takeaways, the book is a must read for anyone who wishes to lead their teams with authenticity.*

—Reggie Rivers, President, The Gala Team

Each Friday brought a bright light and inspirational words from Steve. I found myself looking forward to Fridays. I didn't feel as alone, in my house working . . . we had a shared community at OneCause—all going through this experience together. I remember thanking him for his weekly email, for the positive thoughts and strength both personally and professionally. I appreciated his guidance, thoughtfulness, and advice during the chaos.

—Andrea Kaimowitz (proudly, OneCause)

I always looked forward to Steve's updates. It didn't matter your position, department, or the length of time at OneCause, he spoke to all of us. He reminded us of where the world came from and where it's headed, and that we were and are needed. I valued his perspective that, while we may all be traveling life's path a little differently, we're all on the journey together.

—Stefanie Zachery (proudly, OneCause)

I responded to Steve's updates a couple of times, and I wasn't really expecting a reply. But every time I emailed him, I'd get a response. So the updates were kind of like an open door. He'd share what was going on in his life and in his head, and he'd invite us to share right back. And that sense of connection, that feeling that we're really all together in this, I think that's one of the best things about working at OneCause.

—Brendan Heinz (proudly, OneCause)

DEDICATION

To our Fearless Fundraisers, OneCause Nation, and my steadfast leadership team—thank you. I am grateful for this shared journey and the lessons learned along the way. Day in and day out, you put cause-driven missions at the center of everything you do. Our story is one of resilience, innovation, and teamwork.

To my wife, Sue, who watched me pace, think out loud, and endlessly ideate— you are my partner and confidant in life.

Contents

Author's Note

This book brings together a selection of the updates I shared with my fellow OneCausers across 2020 and 2021. The collection here is not exhaustive, but it does, I believe, provide an honest reflection of the tone of my messages and the challenges tackled across those two tumultuous years.

Each chapter focuses either on moments of particular significance in the OneCause journey through the pandemic or on topics I found especially meaningful, some of which I returned to again and again. The chapters begin with a brief discussion of my motivations for writing a specific update or group of updates and end with some "Leadership Lessons," reflections on leadership that emerged as I wrote, or later re-read, the emails.

At the core of each Chapter are selected updates themselves. These have been lightly edited. From Chapter 2 onward, I have omitted the section of each update that communicated internal company data. Names have been abbreviated or omitted to protect the privacy of team members and OneCause customers.

Prologue

THE WORLD TURNED UPSIDE-DOWN

2020 began as a year full of promise. In January, the OneCause management team sat down for our annual kick-off meeting. Hope, excitement, and powerful momentum were ready to carry us forward.

We knew we could rely on an incredibly talented and committed OneCause team at all levels of the organization. And with our processes refined and tested across a string of high-growth years, well, we were on a roll. Next up—a breakout year in our scale-up journey! As a team, we set ourselves an ambitious goal, one we had never hit before: in 2020, we would help our nonprofits raise a billion dollars for the causes they supported.

It was an opportunity to make a meaningful impact that originally brought me to OneCause. I joined the company in the fall of 2014 at a turning point in my life. During the previous three decades, my career had taken me on a wild ride across the American business landscape. I started out as a trained accountant in financial advisory in the mid-1980s, then side-stepped into the tech sector. I served as an executive at Gateway just in time to see the world reshaped by the rise of home computing and the internet.

By the end of the 1990s, a passion for music led me into the entertainment industry where I worked on everything from digital media platforms to venture capital to live event infrastructure. I even managed a band on the side for awhile! It was a fulfilling career that brought something new onto my desk each morning, and I enjoyed every moment of it. I relished the challenge of building businesses and breaking new ground with technology, and I loved working with creative thinkers, entertainers, and innovators. But as I entered my third decade in the industry, I started to feel there was something missing from my life.

It took a little time to pin the problem down, but once I did, I knew immediately that I needed to make a change. While my work was satisfying, it lacked long-term impact. I was missing a purpose, a mission, a sense of really doing something that mattered for society. So I started looking for an opportunity to use my time and my skills to do some real good in the world. As soon as I met the team at OneCause, I knew I had found my new home.

The mix of product, brand recognition, and growth potential made OneCause an exciting business opportunity. On the surface, this was a chance to do what I had done many times before: help a company grow. But under all the charts, data, and trajectories was something else, an intangible pull, a deeper connection that drew me in.

What made OneCause special was the people and their passion for a vibrant, crystalized mission: to help nonprofits build better tomorrows, one cause at a time.

From my first contact with the company, I was inspired by the commitment of the team and the farsighted vision they rallied around. What they had achieved was already remarkable. OneCause had pioneered a new category of fundraising solutions—mobile bidding—revolutionizing charitable giving. Working with OneCause (or BidPal as we were known when I first came on board) offered the perfect combination of potential, product, and purpose. And so, I set out on this new challenge, full of hope for what we could achieve together.

My love for the people, the business, and our dedicated community of fearless fundraisers grew immensely during my first five years. When we set our billion-dollar fundraising goal in January 2020, I knew it was a big ask. At the same time, I was certain that OneCause Nation would answer the call. We had a deep pool of talent, a goal that mattered, and important missions.

Nothing could stop us.

~

No one who attended our January 2020 meeting mentioned the news reports that were beginning to surface about a health emergency in Wuhan, China. In fact, it wasn't until the end of the month, when the first case of human-to-human transmission was identified in North America, that I found myself giving any real thought to the novel coronavirus. Even then, I didn't dwell on it. While the reports of mass lockdowns and deaths coming out of China were shocking, the United States had just a handful of cases. I couldn't begin to imagine that by the end of the year, nearly 350,000 Americans would be dead.

The 40 days that followed the first locally transmitted US case radically changed the world, OneCause, and our nonprofit customers, as well as the fundraising sector as a whole. Early February saw the emergence of rising hot spots around the country and the introduction of travel restrictions with China. New words like "transmission," "social distancing," "viral spread," and "daily case count" entered the news and our lives. By the end of the month, stock markets around the world were showing a volatility we hadn't seen for years.

As we moved into March, the Centers for Disease Control (CDC) announced that it was preparing for a nationwide outbreak, but life continued largely as normal. Restaurants were open, movie theaters were full, and music fans were enjoying live gigs at venues from coast to coast. Despite the rising tension, it was business as usual in America.

At least we thought it was.

March is affectionately known in nonprofit circles as fundraising "March Madness," the busiest time of the year for charitable events. OneCause had thousands of galas, auctions, and fundraisers on our calendar, with thousands of organizations relying on these events to power their missions. But the second week of March shattered any illusions that our nation, our company, and our fearless fundraisers would escape the growing global crisis. Reality rushed in like a tsunami.

Monday, March 9th saw the biggest single day of stock market losses since the global financial crisis of 2007–2008. While there were still only 1,000 confirmed cases in the US, the complete lockdown in Italy and the rapid spread of the virus in Spain spelled the inevitable truth: exponential spread in America was just a matter of time. The only way to slow the virus was to shut everything down: schools, workplaces, shops, concerts, galas, travel . . . everything.

It seemed crazy, like something out of a dystopian movie. How could daily life just stop for a nation of 300 million people? How could the wheels of the greatest economic engine in history come to a halt? But as the week progressed, it became increasingly clear that something unimaginable was happening.

When the World Health Organization announced on Wednesday, March 11th that COVID was officially a pandemic, the floodgates opened. The NBA suspended its season, MLB Spring Training was cancelled, and the NCAA determined there would be no 2020 Final Four or Tournament.

As we prepared for the biggest event weekend of the year, reality hit nonprofit fundraising squarely in the face. National lockdown had arrived. Customers called from around the country to cancel their fundraising events, some with only a day's notice. It wasn't just the inconvenience of having to change or postpone plans that was unsettling. There was a rising panic in the voices of our fundraising partners.

With the nation shutting down, how would they—how *could* they—find new ways to replace the vital revenue their missions relied on?

When I sat down on Friday (the 13th . . .) to review the situation for the coming weekend, I saw that our live events had dropped to zero. Hundreds of people around the globe were dying from COVID every day.

And this was only the beginning.

CHAPTER 1

When Crisis Comes Knocking

The second half of March 2020 was a time of chaos, confusion, and fear. After weeks of hoping that COVID's impact would be limited, America was waking up to a different reality. While case numbers and deaths were still low, the crisis developing in other countries set expectations about the future. We still didn't know much about the virus, who was at risk, or how it could be stopped. All we knew for certain was that a hard time was coming.

At OneCause, we spent these weeks preparing. On Monday March 16th, the stock market closed to its single biggest point loss in history. This third record-breaking crash in just eight days was a clear signal that economic confidence was plummeting. In the face of the coming storm, nonprofits around the country were making plans, assessing resources, and preserving everything they had for what lay ahead. For us, this meant not just cancellations of upcoming events, but a dramatic slowing of future bookings. Fundraising, for the time being, had stopped.

But OneCause Nation kept going. We searched for ways to support our fearless fundraisers and triage their slashed plans while formulating new ideas that would ultimately evolve into an industry-wide pivot.

In those early days, our teams called thousands of customers, prioritizing their efforts based on event dates. From our sales organization and customer success managers to our fundraising consultants and event success teams as well as support personnel and marketing teams, everyone pitched in. We were determined to help customers reschedule and reimagine virtual versions of their events.

Still, as we lived out our values and pursued our goal of empowering great missions, the unavoidable truth was that we could not sustain the business in this way. It is not an exaggeration to say that our very existence as a company was threatened.

What do you do when a large part of your business model disappears overnight? I knew I wasn't the only person grappling with the question as we moved into the last week of March. There was no playbook for dealing with this kind of crisis, no tried-and-true path back to normalcy. We would have to plot our own course through the storm.

Scary as that thought was, it also gave me confidence. I knew that both OneCause Nation and our fearless customers had the grit and determination necessary to persist and succeed anew. We all had missions that mattered and the passion and commitment to keep moving forward in the face of massive uncertainty. If anyone could steer the ship through the storm to safe harbor, it was the causes we served and the people I worked with every day.

On Monday, March 23rd, our home state of Indiana announced a shelter-in-place order. We had already made working from home an option for all our staff, but the rapid rise of COVID now made it a necessity. With things moving fast, I called the entire company together for a meeting. I knew our employees would be worried about their jobs, their families, and the future of the company. They'd want to know how we planned to do our work without a centralized office and what steps they could take to support our customers at this difficult time. I didn't have all the answers, but I was determined to be transparent and open about where we stood.

It was not an easy presentation. I wanted to be honest about the difficulties we faced while sharing a message of hope. We needed to keep moving forward as a collective team. We needed to not let fear shut us off from the real and urgent needs facing our business and the philanthropy sector.

As a company, we weren't going to cut and run. After meeting with the executive team and our board, we were committed to remaining intact, hunkering down for the long haul, and trimming where we could—but not on the human side of our business.

There would be no mass layoffs, and nobody would lose their benefits. We would move to restructure all aspects of our business—both operationally and financially—in order to give us the maximum runway and preserve precious capital. Most of all, we would continue to be there for our customers no matter what.

There was even some good news to share. Yes, good news in that very first meeting! We were starting to see early signs that the nonprofit sector was adapting, with a large volume of customers contacting us about virtual events and an emerging need for virtual fundraising. Our various products, including our flagship auction and event software, had been enabling remote and online fundraising for years, and we had other tools in the pipeline that had the potential to revolutionize virtual giving. The short-term picture might have been bleak, but there were signs of hope piercing through the gloom.

There was no denying the difficulty of our position, so I decided to share a message filled with reality-based optimism. Yes, the times were uncertain. Yes, it would be tough. But we were going to march forward together as a team and emerge into the post-pandemic world in a position of strength. Missions were riding on us staying the course, as our customers had told us time and time again. I knew it wasn't enough to just say that.

We had to believe, to all have conviction that our work and dedication would continue to make a difference. That meant charting our journey by measuring the recovery of the business through the recovery of the fundraisers we served.

To ensure that everyone could follow the unfolding story on which our business and our jobs depended, I announced I would provide regular company-wide updates. These would communicate how we were doing with straight-shooting facts and data, creating a firm basis for understanding our evolution through this crisis.

And then I went off script . . .

I'm not sure exactly what prompted me, but as I looked up from my notes and met the eyes of the team members on the video call with me, I found myself saying, "And I'm going to do that weekly. I'm going to write those updates to you myself."

As soon as the words were out of my mouth, I thought, "What did I just do?" Putting together a meaningful and detailed update every single week was going to take a lot of time and effort in a period that was exceptionally chaotic. But another part of me could already see the value of frequent and transparent updates. With the company scattered across the country and many teams working from home for the first time, a regular line of communication would be an important tether. It would help me stay linked to every member of the team and give OneCause Nation a common cultural touchpoint that connected us all.

When I sat down to write the first update a week later, I set some guidelines. My immediate goal was to communicate our progress through the pandemic, so we needed data the team could measure that progress against.

I decided to report the number of booked and rescheduled in-person fundraising events, plus the number of cancellations and virtual conversions each week. Comparing these figures with the same data from the first months of the year would enable everyone to track our journey back in a completely transparent way.

I also wanted to share inspiring success stories from our customers to remind everyone about the impact of our work, that what we were doing mattered—now more than ever.

Finally, I wanted to include a personal message to create a connection, a meaningful link to the team in these extraordinary circumstances. I wanted to share my confidence, my hopes, and even my fears. I needed to be honest and open.

So much of the path ahead was shrouded in mist, and false optimism or exaggerated certainty would do nothing to change that. In fact, it would take away from the hard and very real work we had to do. It was important to let everyone know that I was there next to them: unsure and vulnerable but also hopeful and committed.

I didn't have all the answers, but I truly believed that we would find our way through this together.

April 2, 2020

Hey Everyone!

How's it going?

In the pre-COVID world, I used to greet almost everyone like that.

In fact, if I was really feeling my southside of Chicago roots I might have even said, "How ya doin'?" It was really just an expression.

These days when I talk to you, I will purposefully and directly ask you, "How are you?" because I really want to know. I encourage everyone to ask your colleagues, friends, spouse, kids: "How are you?" This crisis is affecting everyone differently.

So . . .

How are you?

Give yourself a break. Give yourself some time.

Last Thursday was tough. It was a hard message to deliver, and I know it was a hard message to hear. But the responses I received, and the grit I have seen demonstrated since then have been nothing less than inspirational!

Thank you for all of your words of support, gratitude, and recommitment to OneCause.

We are in this together. We will get through this together.

But it's not just going to happen. We have to *make it happen*.

I made a commitment to a weekly update, and so here is my first weekly update:

We had 167 events originally scheduled for the week of 3/22. Here's what has happened to those 167 events:

- 32 Converted to Virtual (19%)
- 12 Postponed (7%)
- 97 Date moved out/rescheduled to new date (58%)
- 19 Cancelled (12%)
- 7 Undetermined (4%)

The good news on cancellations is still holding. Great work to everyone who has been in contact with a customer who is confused, scared, and looking for guidance. "We got this." We still have the opportunity for events that have either postponed or moved their date out! I keep saying this is a timing/temporary difference. Not a permanent one. Let's ask ourselves, how can we take them virtual?!

FEARLESS FUNDRAISING IN ACTION

Thanks to the tireless and creative work from our teams this past week, we were able to help 32 organizations execute virtual fundraisers.

Below are a few highlights:

- JDRF Virginia was able to shift their Denim and Diamonds Gala to a successful virtual event, surpassing their goal through an online auction, donation appeal, and raffle.
- The Academy of Holy Names had rave reviews about our resources and teams (especially Missy) as their virtual Black & White By The Bay Gala "could not have gone any better." They achieved 109% of silent auction proceeds to value!
- Thanks to the team's (especially Sara A's) "ingenuity and guidance," Our Lady of Good Counsel was able to seamlessly move their event online with more than 450 donors to reach a record raised.

QUOTE OF THE WEEK

"OneCause saved us. If we didn't have the auction virtually, we would have had to cancel the entire event. We were able to make our goal all online. Thank you!"

—Sheena, Director of Annual Giving & Special Events, Benjamin School

Our customers say it best, don't they?

There you have it. Our first weekly update in the COVID world. Stay safe. Stay healthy. Do good.

Drop me a note to tell me how you're doing. I want to know.

Onward,

Steve

April 9, 2020

Hi OneCause!

Can it really be Thursday again? Well, happy Thursday then!

I know that you all are moving mountains to take care of our customers, and I **thank you** for that. I know that many of our customers are still paralyzed in their thoughts and actions. They need us now more than ever.

One local nonprofit customer that I'd like to highlight this week is decidedly NOT paralyzed in their thoughts or actions.

Second Helpings has risen to the occasion—providing for the increased need of the food insecure in Indianapolis. They've also taken their annual Corks & Forks fundraising gala from its usual venue, Bankers Life Arena, to an online auction and virtual event.

To meet the increased demand due to the COVID crisis, Second Helpings has doubled the number of hot meals they prepare for the area's shelters and food pantries to 50,000 per week. If you want inspiration for how to rise above your current situation, count your own blessings, and take action to help others:

"$5.00 provides a dinner for four."

That's easy math. Easy to understand IMPACT.

What we're doing to help our customers is *more important than ever.*

I established something of a format in last week's inaugural update, so I'll try to stick to that to give you some consistency of reported information.

We had 211 events originally scheduled for the week beginning 3/30 and ending 4/5. Here's what has happened to those 211 events:

- 50 Converted to Virtual (24%)
- 24 Postponed without a new date or unresolved (11%)
- 117 Date moved out/rescheduled to new date (55%)
- 20 Cancelled (9.5%)

Cancellations are still holding. Continued great work by everyone who has been in contact with a customer on what to do next. We've been playing a little catch-up here, but I feel that we're turning the corner and getting out in front of this. The answer might not be a virtual gala. The answer might be peer-to-peer or online giving campaigns. Let's create a new category—Converted to Peer-to-Peer. The thing to remember is: "We got this." We have a solution for those unmet fundraising needs.

FEARLESS FUNDRAISING IN ACTION

As you can see from above, last week we were able to convert 50 events into online or virtual fundraisers from what were originally in-person galas or auction events. Peer-to-Peer events are also taking the spotlight with the emergence of "virtual bowling!" Below are a few highlights:

- St. Louis University High School rallied their community for #Cashbah2020 with virtually hosted happy hours based on table assignments, pre-recorded impact videos with families and alumni, a packed silent auction, and a livestreamed fund-a-need on Facebook Live. The virtual event raised an unprecedented amount in support of financial aid.
- The 2020 ForkKids Art Auction: Abracadabra continues to raise money beyond this past weekend to meet their Fund-a-Need Reverse Auction Goal and to bring in an

additional matching gift. Their silent auction alone was impressive, achieving 364% of value with all funds going toward homeless services to families in Virginia.

- Big Brothers Big Sisters of Dane County successfully pivoted their signature bowling event to the Virtual Bowl for Kids' Sake. The campaign includes weekly activity and fundraising challenges that kicked off on Monday. Virtual bowling events take place April–May. So far, the campaign has attracted more than 244 participants and solid fundraising!
- St. Monica Academy went all in with their Casino Royale Galathon Livestream, complete with recommended themed attire, live music, menus, and cocktail recipes for family "viewing parties." The virtual event was a huge success through their silent auction, raffle drawings, and virtual paddle raise.

QUOTE(S) OF THE WEEK

*"Our gala is our biggest revenue generator of the year. We have to have the event. Without it, we can't fund tuition assistance which 60% of our families rely on. To say we were freaking out is an understatement. But we divided and conquered and made it happen. **Anyone can do this!**"*

—Karen, *Development Director, Holy Cross High School*

"We LOVE OneCause Peer-to-Peer! If we had not moved our walk from our previous provider to you, going virtual would have never been an option."

—Nathan, *Vice President of Philanthropy, RAIN*

I wanted to add this one to show you the mentality of the donor/ organization relationship:

The founder of GiGi's Playhouse had a donor tell her this:

"It is not your choice to make—whether to donate or not—you just have to choose to keep asking."

Our customers (and their donors) still say it best.

Well, that's it for this week.

I miss you guys. I miss seeing everyone from out of town visiting the Indy office. I miss walking the halls and saying, "Hey." I miss stopping by your desk to chat. I miss the buzz of our team helping new customers get set up for fundraising success. I miss meeting in person, and I miss whiteboards. I miss Friday donuts. ☺

We will get back to [new] normal again.

We will get through this. We will get through this together.

Onward,

Steve

LEADERSHIP LESSONS

- **Honesty matters**

  When your organization is facing an existential threat, the only path that will carry you through intact is one that brings your team with you. Unrealistic projections and lofty promises are cheap tricks that devalue your most important asset: an authentic connection with the people you rely on. If you are honest and open about the situation and the path forward, everyone knows where they stand and what needs to be done.

- **Adapt to meet the difficulties at hand**

  When a crisis comes knocking, it's no use hoping that "more of the same" methods and processes will provide a viable way forward. You need to be ready to rebuild systems and procedures from scratch to adapt to the new reality. And remember, you're not just playing a defensive game. Survival through the crisis is the baseline. Your real goal is to develop plans that will help you thrive and emerge stronger.

- **Share strong and simple messages of hope**

  As a leader, it's your role to be a beacon of hope, no matter how hard the situation. It's okay to be honest and vulnerable, but never allow yourself to be bowed down or defeated. Share positive messages about the future, even if they only provide a glimmer of optimism. Talk about the future and lean into your mission. Even in the face of uncertainty, let your team and your customers (and supporters) know, "We got this!"

- **Remember what's important**

  There is no better source of resolution and grit in the face of difficulties than the reminder that what you do is important—that your efforts, your mission, and your work matter. Draw on this assurance to keep yourself moving forward and find channels to broadcast and share it with your team. As a bonus, the team will know how valuable and appreciated their work is.

CHAPTER 2

No Mud, No Lotus

We moved into the second half of April with a sense of both trepidation and relief. One of the most tumultuous months of our lives lay behind us, a whirlwind of confusion and chaos without parallel. But despite the feeling that we were only just setting out into an unknown future, the existential threat of the first weeks of the pandemic had receded. We had made it through the initial crisis, and there was now time to catch our collective breath.

As the situation began to stabilize, I found myself thinking about the task I had taken on when I promised to write a company-wide update every week. Full disclosure: I was concerned. I wasn't worried about running out of material. Far from it. OneCause was changing faster and more radically than ever, with each day accelerating the evolution of our teams, our processes, and the ways in which nonprofits were using our products. There was plenty to talk about. What worried me was that I might not have anything practical or helpful to share.

The last thing I wanted to do was drop a time-suck into everyone's inboxes every week. We all had enough to work through and adapt to already without having to carve out time for empty words. If my updates kept people busy without providing inspiration, insight, or emotional support, they would be worse than useless.

The first weeks of the pandemic had been so chaotic and threatening that I reached an important conclusion. The best way to support the team was clear: communicate honestly, with a firm hopefulness about the difficulties we were facing and the steps we were taking to meet them. This was "Titanic" mode. Danger was staring us in the face, and it was my responsibility as CEO to get everyone into the lifeboats as quickly and safely as possible. *Put the life preserver on . . . Make some room there . . . Pick up an oar . . . Help those around you . . .*

It was disaster leadership and communication. The decisions we were making and the messages we were sharing aimed to accomplish two things: keep us and our fearless fundraisers afloat and hustle us through to the next essential action. But now that we began to adjust to the reality of the pandemic, we needed a different approach.

I had no idea how long we would be in this new boat—there was no timetable or roadmap for navigating the journey—but I knew it would be months at the very least. And sustaining our people beyond the short term would take more than just information and instruction. We needed a vision, an anchor, and a way of thinking that would help us move forward together.

I wanted to provide tools that would help our teams do more than just survive. We needed to come out of this terrible situation unbowed and carrying glimmers of real positivity. After all, our existence as an organization wasn't the only thing that mattered. It wasn't even the most important part of our business. We had thousands of nonprofits, thousands of other teams across North America that were relying on *us* to provide them with the tools they needed to keep powering their missions. Our responsibility to those nonprofits and the causes they served was immense. We had to find enough strength to move forward and deliver the best possible outcomes for them.

I was lying on my stretching mat one morning, listening to my Calm® app, when I heard a story about how the lotus flower only exists because of the muck of the pond. Without that muddy darkness below the water, without the struggle to reach the surface, there would be no beautiful flower. As soon as I heard the story, something clicked. It was perfect. It reflected exactly the message I wanted to get across in a relatable and interesting way.

When I sat down to write that week's update, what emerged was very different from previous weeks. I wrote about the lotus, about how inspirational its journey was, and how it mirrored the challenges we faced. I tried to be open and vulnerable, to encourage people to explore these ideas with me. No one had the answers in those early days. Everyone was tense, scared, and in need of a bigger story to connect to. What I wanted to communicate was that we might be in the mud now, but we *would* find a way through, and we *would* be better for it.

By sharing the lotus story, I would put myself on the page. I would offer a different way of seeing our current situation and challenges, a perspective that might help us face them and move through them as a team. It felt good. It felt honest. I was finding my voice.

Then I worried that I was writing about finding something positive in the pandemic when some people were losing so much. I worried that my teams were looking for a rock of certainty and might lose faith if their CEO didn't have all the answers. I worried that there were 300+ OneCausers, each with different burdens, who might need to hear something completely different.

Pushing past these concerns, I hit Send. If the pandemic was teaching me anything, it was that we all have fears, and we have to live with them and act in spite of them. Hiding, waiting, and hoping for a different outcome isn't an option. There will always be darkness, but pushing through adversity paves the way for the light that follows.

April 16, 2020

no mud. no lotus.

Each morning, *every morning*, I set my phone's clock timer for 20 minutes. The first ten minutes are spent with the "Daily Calm" found on the Calm app. Each session starts with a focus on breathing and mindfulness and ends with a daily message. My second ten minutes are spent doing light exercise and stretching.

This morning, I was deep in thought—with COVID taking its usual place of prominence at the top of my list. But, of course, the key to mindfulness and meditation is to "push thoughts away" and focus on the breath. Have you ever tried that? It's really hard.

My personal best is probably 15 seconds. They call it "practice" for a reason. ☺

The message this morning was just what I needed. I decided to share it with you as today's theme.

No mud. No lotus.

Paraphrasing a bit here . . . *The lotus begins its life in the mud of a pond and gradually pushes through the muck and darkness to the surface and in time rises up on top of the water as its leaves and flower bloom forth for the sun's warmth and light.*

Just as the lotus must push through the mud and darkness, we must push through our setbacks, suffering, and loss to grow and emerge to realize our full potential.

Fight through adversity. Face suffering without being hurt by it. Our difficulties are part of our journey. Face your challenge. Adversity gives way to growth and wisdom.

Face discomfort and move through it.

Our current hardship can be a source of growth and transformation.

Deep stuff I know, but *I'm growing too!*

For those of you looking for less spiritual guidance, I'd also like to share some guidance I read from Boston Consulting Group in the *Harvard Business Review*:

*"Efficiency reigns in a stable world with no surprises, and this mindset is often dominant in large corporations. But the key goal in managing dynamic and unpredictable challenges is **resilience**—the ability to survive and thrive through unpredictable, changing, and potentially unfavorable events."*

—Harvard Business Review (Business History, February 27, 2020): "Lead Your Business Through the Coronavirus Crisis" by Martin Reeves, Nikolaus Lang, and Philipp Carlsson-Szlezak

This describes our situation pretty well, doesn't it? The authors offered six characteristics of "resilient" systems or behaviors. I've listed them below with a few notes of my own. I challenge you to think about how you can apply these characteristics every day.

1. **Redundancy.** Your backup plans need to have backup plans. Plan B is not enough. Look beyond the traditional.
2. **Diversity.** Think differently. Get a variety of inputs and opinions. Think multi-dimensionally. There's more than one way to solve a problem. Since you're home, ask your loved ones for their advice and input.
3. **Modularity.** BidPal is a monolith. Our new Fundraising Platform is modular. If one piece breaks down, you can work around it or swap it out without taking the whole system down. Our fundraising solutions are modular. Online Fundraising. Text2Give. Find what works.
4. **Evolvability.** We have to be flexible. There is more unknown than known. Let's try some stuff. We're going to get some things wrong, but we'll learn and change our approach. Over time, we'll figure it out. Over time, we will see more clearly.

5. **Prudence.** Considering the extent of the unknown, we have to apply rational thinking and judgment to our forward-looking models. We can hope that our customers get "back to the ballroom" soon, but we have to develop plans for a less optimistic scenario.

6. **Embeddedness.** Granted, we don't use this term very often, but it is good to think about. We are part of a broader community. Our decisions and approach need to consider the impacts they have on our customers, partners, and colleagues. Just because we're in crisis mode, we can't forget our values. Now is the time we look to our values even more than ever.

Both approaches have a common theme—**embrace the adversity, fight through, and grow.**

FEARLESS FUNDRAISING IN ACTION

- The Brownell Talbot College Preparatory School had huge success with their 68132 Virtual Gala through their online auction and donation appeal. Throughout the weekend they brought their Beverly Hills 90210 theme to life and drove supporter engagement with fun memes and pre-recorded videos from alumni, students, staff, and even a special social media appeal from Tori Spelling and a drop-in from Gabrielle Carteris during their Virtual Gala Zoom.

- Cancer Wellness Center (CWC) originally planned to hold its annual Stepping Up to Wellness Run/Walk on April 26th. However, in the face of the COVID pandemic, they decided to move to a virtual race allowing supporters to participate with a self-paced race that can be completed anywhere—treadmill, track, or trail—until May 26th. They are well on their way to meeting their goal, signing up 190 participants in their first week!

- The Bear Creek School kicked off their Come Together Online Auction on Tuesday and have already done exceedingly well in silent auction proceeds in the first 48 hours (at 105% of auction value). Additionally, they have an interesting tidbit. They are in Redmond, WA, probably one of the first and hardest hit centers of the pandemic. All proceeds will go towards creating the Bear Creek Responds Grant Fund to help offset unanticipated immediate tuition needs and ensure that these families remain part of their school community.

OneCause Teams in Action

- We had more than *8,800 registrants* for our webinars in response to COVID over the past 30 days!
- Great work by the consulting and event success teams—contacting more than **1,700 customers** to determine their "Event Contingency Status" and move more than 20% into "Virtual"—with a goal of hitting 45% by summer with the assist of the customer success and sales teams.

QUOTE OF THE WEEK

"I just want to say thank you to you and your team at OneCause for providing nonprofit employees with these excellent, helpful, and free webinars on a variety of important fundraising initiatives. During this unprecedented time of the COVID pandemic, it is so nice to know I have the opportunity to keep my skills fresh and up to date with OneCause webinars. In addition, I feel like I have a friend, some company, by attending the sessions. Thanks, again, for all of us out here who are worried, frightened, and scared about

NO MUD, NO LOTUS

the future of our profession and the future of all the nonprofits who provide such outstanding services to their communities."

—S. Helper (yep, that's her real name!), Professional Fundraiser

In order to emerge victorious, we still need to:

- Keep delivering the highest level of customer experience.
- Keep finding creative solutions for our customers.
  - Virtual
  - Online
  - Peer-to-Peer
- Keep our expenses low.
- Keep building awesome new products.
- Keep supporting our customers and preparing them for their events.
- Keep doing what OneCause does best—take care of our customers!!
- Keep taking care of each other.

It's been quite a week. I hope you're still doing OK working from home. I know that I am always in the way with my "home office" spread out all over the kitchen/living room. Our lives continue to be massively disrupted, but all I see and hear of is continual, relentless, and positive action from every one of you. Thank you.

My apologies for the length of this update, but I had a lot to say! Wishing you and your loved ones health, happiness, and safety! 'Til next week.

. . . and with apologies to USC for stealing their motto . . .

Fight on!

Steve

LEADERSHIP LESSONS

- **Adversity is a seed**
  No matter how dark the situation, the struggle to overcome difficulty shapes us. When we become conscious of the possibilities offered by adversity, we can draw on it as a resource to hone ourselves and develop our potential. Just like the lotus, beauty, growth, and life can come from the darkest of places.

- **Honesty and uncertainty are sources of strength**
  A good leader needs to balance optimism and confidence about the future with honesty about the challenges that lay in the path ahead. When things are tough, and there is no clear path forward, tell your team the truth. Even when you are unsure, tell them you don't know, but that you are confident you can and will figure it out together. Real strength comes from identifying challenges, sharing your thoughts as they evolve, and inviting the team to think through the challenges with you.

- **We are all leaders**
  Organizations that value creativity and problem solving don't divide themselves into leaders and followers. Everyone has the aptitude, ability, and responsibility to lead. And everyone is accountable for marshalling the organization's resources and helping to make decisions that move our causes forward. The best way through a crisis is to empower everyone to identify where they can make a difference.

CHAPTER 3

Staying Stoic

No Mud, No Lotus set the tone for many of the OneCause updates during the next two years. It didn't serve as a template, and it wasn't until months later that I was truly comfortable with my voice. Still, the combination of abstract ideas, practical tools, and openness about shared challenges provided a framework I returned to often.

The idea of fighting through adversity to build something better and emerge into the light sparked touching and often very personal responses from the team. It was incredibly moving to hear from OneCausers across the country about how the message had resonated with them. But as I began to write my next update, I was conscious that we couldn't expect the lotus to blossom any time soon.

On TV and in the print and digital media, most commentators seemed to think the pandemic would be over in a flash: a few weeks of sacrifice, and we'd be back to normal with barely a scratch. While optimism and a positive outlook are essential, their flawed assumptions were playing out in daily case counts, ongoing stay-at-home orders, and the continued disruption of our public life.

At this point, we really didn't know how long COVID would be with us. The only thing that was clear was that it was here, and it wasn't going away soon. It had taken more than two years for the Spanish Flu that began toward the end of World War I to burn itself out. And if history was any guide, we couldn't assume that the first wave would be the worst. We needed to prepare for the long haul and ready ourselves for the possibility that we would be struggling through the mud for a while. As for how long it would take . . . we just did not know.

When I read this quote from British philosopher Bertrand Russell, I knew right away how to begin my next update:

> "The whole problem with the world is that fools and fanatics are always so certain of themselves, and wiser people so full of doubts."
> Bertrand Russell

These lines were the reminder we all needed not to take the talking heads too seriously. We needed to flow with the uncertainty rather than make assumptions about how the pandemic would end. We needed to manage our lives, intentions, and mindsets so that our happiness wouldn't depend on events we couldn't control. As I thought about Russell's words, it became clear to me that one way of getting through these challenges was to stay stoic.

The word "stoic" has had a long journey through ancient Greek and Latin and into the English language where it has come to mean "unemotional" or "without passion." That's not a model for living that interests me. Without passion, we have no fire. Without emotions, we cut ourselves off from other people.

But the origins of *stoic* have another story to tell. Starting more than 2000 years ago, the Stoic philosophers taught their contemporaries how to be rational, use reason to understand the world, and avoid getting trapped by false beliefs about what is in our power. In this sense of the word, to be stoic is to engage with the world as it really is, without being overwhelmed by it.

I was introduced to the Stoics when a business associate gave me a copy of Marcus Aurelius' *Meditations*. *Meditations* had been on my "I'll get around to it" list since college. I knew only that it was a classic. So, when the gift showed up in my mailbox, I started leafing through to see what all the fuss was about. A few minutes later, I was gripped. There was so much engaging and accessible wisdom on the pages in front of me that it was hard to put down.

Marcus Aurelius wrote nearly two millennia ago, yet despite all those centuries between us, what he had to say resonated deeply. As the emperor of Rome, he had plenty to be stressed about including invasions, rebellions, financial troubles, famines, and one of the worst pandemics in history. In 165 AD, Marcus Aurelius' Roman Empire was hit with the Antonine Plague which would claim the lives of an estimated 5 to 10 million people.

Despite all this, he put his Stoic worldview to work, writing as just another human who had to deal with the uncertainty and difficulties everyone faces. His reflections have a universal character, and they speak to us now as much as they did to his contemporaries.

The Stoics believed that the most important task all humans face is working out how to be happy in a world we don't control. Their essential view is that while we can't control what takes place in the world at large, we *can* command how we respond to events. Our responses are *always* up to us! Stoic thinkers—both the ancients like Marcus Aurelius and more modern supporters like Ryan Holiday—offer all sorts of insights to help us realize what is—and isn't—in our power. Armed with this vital distinction, we can set aside some of the biggest sources of stress we face.

Even before COVID began, the Stoics had become one of my go-to resources for inspiration or a fresh perspective. But when COVID turned up on our doorsteps to remind us just how much of our world is beyond our control, their ideas seemed more valuable than ever.

We were all dealing with a huge amount of stress. Rather than pretend that the cares of the world were sliding off my back, I wanted to acknowledge that I was struggling too. By sharing the tools that were helping me, I hoped to offer the OneCause Nation something of practical value while kickstarting conversations about how we could deal with the unpredictable reality we were all facing.

After sending the update, I was amazed to learn just how many other OneCausers already had an interest in Stoicism! Even more gratifying was the positive feedback from people who hadn't encountered this world-view before. Enthused by the response, I returned to the theme a month later with an update focused on Marcus Aurelius. As the year progressed, Stoic thinkers and ideas became a regular feature in my writing.

At OneCause, our staff and the customers we serve include Buddhists, Hindus, and Muslims, members of Christian and Jewish organizations, atheists and agnostics, and supporters of many other belief systems. There is no single faith that holds us together, no single creed or confession that binds us. But Stoicism offers something we can all make use of, something we can all fit into our belief system without raising barriers or digging ditches. While I took care not to lean on it too heavily, I loved that it provided a touchpoint for all of us.

April 23, 2020

Hey OneCause!

Really, what's better than these weekly Thursday updates from Steve? I know.

How about 1/2 hour live on Monday morning??!

Earlier in the week, you received an email reserving 11-11:30 am ET next Monday the 27th. I look forward to sharing some of the same type of updates with you then—only live! So, no Thursday update this week.

In the meantime, I did want to share this nugget which is so perfect for these times we are living through. It's confusing and conflicting to hear the various plans for getting out of our homes, getting back to work, and getting our economy going again.

My trusty Calm app served up this morsel this morning:

> *"The whole problem with the world is that fools*
> *and fanatics are always so certain of themselves,*
> *and wiser people so full of doubts."*
>
> *—Bertrand Russell*

There is still so much uncertainty with the current COVID situation.

Be wary of anyone who believes they know the answers. Be thoughtful. Be mindful. Be analytical. Be reasonable.

As I was writing this, another quote came to mind. I don't remember the first time I heard it, and Google attributes it to half a dozen sources. Where exactly it comes from doesn't matter. It goes something like this:

> *"We can't control the events of the world, but we*
> *can control how we respond to them."*

The ancient Greek Stoic philosopher Epictetus said something similar:

"It's not what happens to you, but how you react to it that matters."
Epictetus

Enjoy your weekend! Looking forward to connecting with you on Monday morning!

Be safe, be healthy.

Steve

May 28, 2020

Hey Team OneCause!

Man, I did NOT see this coming. I don't believe that anyone did. We're now coming to the end of our 11th week of "shelter in place."

There is good news! We're starting to see the light at the end of the tunnel. At least for now. Our home state of Indiana is in Phase 3 of our reopening, which began on May 24th with:

- Acceptable gathering of up to 100 people with social distancing protocols applied.
- Continued encouragement to work from home.
- Restaurants open at 50% capacity.
- Retail and malls open at 75% capacity.
- Gyms and fitness centers open with strict guidelines.

- 65 and older and other "at risk" people should self-limit their exposure at all times.

Other states, cities, and counties across the US are following their own "back on track" protocols. Amid this hope, there is still worry. There is still concern. Are we rushing in? Are we not paying attention to the warning signs?

Do you find yourself saying . . .

"I'm following the PPE guidelines, but no one else is."

"I still feel at risk."

"I'm stressed."

I know.

It seems like we're all trying to do more these days. But it also seems like we have even *less time* to do more. We're only working four days a week. We're working from our kitchen tables, home offices, couches, and anywhere we can get some peace and quiet. Some of us are also homeschooling, feeding, and entertaining our kids.

It is stressful.

There are many online resources for tips on dealing with stress. I would encourage you to do some searching. There are a lot of good ideas.

I'd like to share one that is a couple of thousand years old. I've quoted Marcus Aurelius in the past. How did I meet Marcus? Someone I had just met and was sharing a meal with sized me up in a couple of hours and said, "Steve, I have a book for you." They ordered it on Amazon right at the dinner table and a few days later, I received *Meditations* by Marcus Aurelius. Eight bucks on Amazon right now. Invest in yourself. Guaranteed you will learn $8 worth, or I will refund your money! Send me the receipt.

So, what does this guy know about stress? Marcus Aurelius was the Emperor of Rome. He was invaded, survived a palace coup, had stomach problems, more war, floods, famine, and a pandemic. He was also a philosopher in the school of "Stoicism."

There are so many great quotes, but here are some words of wisdom for all of us:

"If you seek tranquility, do less."

But then he makes a critical clarification:

*"Or (more accurately) do what's essential . . .
Because most of what we say and do is not essential.
If you can eliminate it, you'll have more time."*

We're all trying to do more with less time. Keep the words of Marcus Aurelius in mind as you plan your day. Ask yourself, "What is essential?" Focus on that and get it done. Eliminate the non-essential. Give yourself the gift of more time.

FEARLESS FUNDRAISING IN ACTION

Here's a great customer story to inspire us and remind us of our purpose:

Prairie School—Premiere 2020

The Prairie School brought the ballroom to the virtual world with their Virtual Premiere 2020 over the weekend including an online auction, short video program, and donation appeal. Using OneCause Auction and Event Software, they organized fun with Zoom cocktails, suggested local food, and themed virtual backgrounds. They went above and beyond to educate donors and supporters about the move to virtual with "Virtual Premiere 101" infographics and a "How to Bid" tab in their Giving Center site. Their efforts paid off in silent auction proceeds and total revenue by the end of the event!

QUOTE OF THE WEEK

"With OneCause, making the switch to virtual was easy. We can't wait to incorporate everything we learned this year with online giving. It expanded our reach, and our fundraising really benefited from that."

—Emily, Director of Communications, Wayland Academy

We're literally writing the book as we go. There is no manuscript. There is no playbook.

With focus, we'll be back stronger than ever.

Special thanks goes out to the spouses, significant others, children, loved ones, friends, and all who are putting up with us! My wife has to listen to me every day. ☺ She and all our loved ones are in it with us! Please express to them my gratitude.

Best,

Steve

December 12, 2020

chess.

I'm willing to bet there will be a lot of chess sets under the Christmas tree this year. What's driving that? Netflix's "The Queen's Gambit." Turns out the "Queen's Gambit" has nothing to do with Netflix's other hit "The Crown" (about the Queen and the royal family) but is rather the description of an opening move (followed by a series of prescribed moves) in chess.

Sue and I are doing a slow roll through the series (and we haven't finished it yet, so please no spoilers), but the quote below from Beth really struck me as we watched. I thought to myself, "I'm going to use that in my weekly update." ☺

> *"Chess isn't always competitive. Chess can also be beautiful. It was the board I noticed first. It's an entire world of just 64 squares. I feel safe in it. I can control it. I can dominate it. And it's predictable, so if I get hurt, I only have myself to blame."*
> Beth Harmon, The Queen's Gambit

You see, I've seen so many references to "chess as a reflection of life" and "chess as life" that I couldn't help but think of the opposite. Beth feels safe in chess. Life is not safe. Life includes chaos. The unknown. The unexpected. The unpredictable.

Yes, there are so many things that you can learn by playing chess. To pay someone a compliment, you say, "She's very strategic. She's like a chess player."

The list doesn't stop there. Chess can help you:

1. Improve concentration.

2. Plan several moves ahead.

3. Improve your memory.

4. Make sacrifices for the greater good.

5. Make better decisions and manage your time.

6. Be strategic and tactical.

7. Be creative.

8. The list goes on.

Chess is great. Don't get me wrong.

But let's look at what Beth said again, "*It's an entire world of just 64 squares. I feel safe in it. I can control it. I can dominate it. And it's predictable, so if I get hurt, I only have myself to blame.*"

Our world has virtually *no boundaries.* COVID has taught us that threats can present themselves from the other side of the world in the course of days/weeks/months. Life is totally unpredictable. It's like someone came by your chess game and took a blowtorch to a knight, a bishop, and a few pawns and calmly said, "Play on." You're like, "Huh? What? That's not fair! How can we ever feel safe??"

Also, in chess you know what each piece is allowed to do. There are rules on which direction you move and how many spaces they can move. You take turns playing for goodness sake!! This is nothing like real life.

Back to Beth. She understands this. She doesn't see chess as a metaphor for life. She sees chess as a way to *organize the chaos that is her life.* She brings order to where there is none. She uses chess as something that she can control because she knows she can't control life. She feels safe playing chess.

Lack of control can lead to a feeling of overwhelm. Overwhelm leads to worry and anxiety.

We can't control life, but we can (like Beth and like chess) develop strategies for overcoming the stress that the chaos and uncertainty of life can create. We can control how we respond to this uncertainty and create a sense of safety:

1. Simplify your life.
    a. Streamline your space. Don't wait for the spring. Get rid of stuff right now. Look around you. What doesn't need to be there? Clear it out. 1-800-GOT-JUNK.
    b. Declutter your mind. Meditate. Mindfulness. Journal. Make lists. Get stuff done. There's nothing better than checking off "to dos."
2. Play chess!
    a. Truly. Look at the list I provided above. Chess does not equal life. It's a tool to help you create order in chaos.
3. Sit in the quiet and still your mind.
    a. Leave your phone in a drawer for at least one hour. Yikes!
    b. I heard a great quote from my Calm app last week: "*Mindfulness is the space between Stimulus and Response.*" That really made me stop and think. We live in a stimulus-response world. Add some peace and quiet in between.
4. Let go of negative thoughts.
    a. "*Turn your wounds into wisdom.*" —Oprah
    b. Get away from negative people.
5. Practice a growth mindset and learn something new.
    a. I've always said that I wanted to learn Italian. I'm going to do it. Starting today.
    b. Check me on it.

These actions are all consistent with "creating a safe space" (like Beth). I found a couple of inspiring quotes on this. Agapi Stassinopoulos is an inspirational author. She says:

> *"The world can only seem a safe place when we feel safe inside."*
> Agapi Stassinopoulos

And from the Stoics, whom I haven't gone to in some time, Marcus Aurelius said:

> *"You have power over your mind not outside events, realize this and you will find strength."*
> Marcus Aurelius

You've seen variations on this theme in my weekly updates before. That's because it's important. It's important to know that we face uncertainty, stress, and anxiety about today and what is yet to come.

We've been living in a world that no one asked or planned for. Yet, we have to find strategies to overcome the obstacles that have been placed in our way.

These strategies you can practice on your own. But sometimes you might need some help.

As we are now approaching the end of the year and the holidays, I want to strongly encourage everyone to take a moment to assess your physical and emotional wellness. The New Year will not be a panacea for the trials of 2020, but it *will* be our reward for persevering through 2020!

Take a beat. Sit a moment. Collect your thoughts and make a plan.

I need all of you to be healthy and ready. Be prepared for what could be a breakout year for OneCause!

Virtual. Hybrid. Integrated Fundraising Platform. In-person events. Confidence. Return to growth!

Let's go!

FEARLESS FUNDRAISING IN ACTION

Each week, I am inspired by and in awe of our customers. They are resilient and creative. This week is no exception. Please take some time and read through these success stories. There may be inspiration here that you could use to help an existing customer get "unstuck" and take action.

Ashland Theatre—Holiday Spectacular

Ashland Theatre hosted its inaugural Holiday Spectacular this past weekend streaming live from their theatre in North Carolina. The evening featured a telethon and musical performances with a live and "shhhh" (silent) auction. They also raised funds through a Barrel of Booze raffle including a private label Bourbon. According to the Ashland Theatre team, the evening was a "smashing success" raising much-needed funds for the Ashland Theatre Foundation, with a Live Auction still to come. Funds raised will go to support the theatre's efforts to serve the Ashland community and continue to bring people around the commonwealth together.

QUOTE OF THE WEEK

"I loved working with OneCause. Rebecca and Stacy were AMAZING to work with. When we had some communication issues occur during a role change the entire OneCause team helped fix it and the response was pretty immediate. In the days leading up to the event, the OneCause team was so kind and helpful and knowledge-able. I have been recommending you all to all the other nonprofits I work with."

—Madeleine, Campaign Development Manager, Leukemia and Lymphoma Society—California Southland

Be safe!

Steve

LEADERSHIP LESSONS

- **Focus on what's in your power**
  Concentrating on the things you can change, and accepting the things you cannot, free up valuable energy to strive toward achievable goals. These practices also help you maintain a healthy disposition in a world that can often seem chaotic and unmanageable. When things around you are in turmoil and the times are changing, find those few truths or paths that can make an impact and rally others around them.

- **Put your own mask on first**
  We have the greatest control over what goes on in our own minds. Start from there and work outward. When we change our own mindsets, we reduce our stress levels, increase our health and happiness, and improve our ability to serve others. Be the change by modeling the change for others.

CHAPTER 4

No Room on the Sidelines

I spent the last week of May 2020 on vacation in Florida with my wife. I'd been reminding the OneCause team of the need to pause, reflect, and take meaningful breaks, but I hadn't been practicing what I was preaching. So, we decided to unplug and recharge at a long-time family getaway spot: Cocoa Beach. The plan was to travel there for the Memorial Day holiday and swap COVID-driven news bulletins for relaxation, good company, and some reading and reflection.

The high point of the week came the following Saturday when we watched the first manned rocket launch from Cape Canaveral since the end of the Space Shuttle program in 2011. It was a powerful moment. The beach was covered with families and couples, some wearing masks—others not, everyone stood at a distance from one another, kept apart by the virus at an event that would normally find us standing shoulder to shoulder.

Despite the distance, there was a feeling of community. We were gathered to watch an incredible display of innovation and technology, a demonstration of what this country can achieve when we work together. People were waving American flags, and some were crying. It was emotional, this feeling of being together despite the space that separated us. After months of living apart in a social bubble, it reminded me of the whole we all belong to. It reminded me of the connections that bind us together as a nation.

Later that day, I was flipping through the channels looking for coverage of the launch when I caught a fragment of news. Something was happening in Minneapolis . . . people on the streets . . . protests . . . *Breaking News* banners rolled across the screen. At first, I didn't process what was going on. We were on a family vacation and I had unplugged for a bit.

The tragedy of George Floyd's death which had actually occurred on May 25, Memorial Day 2020, and the scale of the upheaval that followed became a reality for me that Monday morning. It was a stark reminder that, however interconnected some of us might feel, others struggle every day with the long-term effects of racial injustice, exclusion, and bias.

We at OneCause weren't just observers. We had team members in the Minneapolis–Saint Paul area who were intimately affected. And we had nonprofit partners there who were dedicated to community engagement, inclusivity, and fighting systemic racism. Across both the OneCause team and the country as a whole, the emotions unleashed were intense: a combination of outrage, frustration, and heartbreak. It felt as if we as a people were not living out our own ideals.

In my inbox that Monday morning was an email sent late the previous night by a OneCauser from the Twin Cities. Highlighting the devastating effect of the recent events on her local community, she challenged OneCause to take "the opportunity for us all to stop and examine ourselves and our organization." She signed off, "Sleepless in St. Paul."

Her message was a challenge to change, and a catalyst. We took some initial steps in the days that followed. We let our nonprofit partners know we stood against injustice, prejudice, and inequality. And we let them know we stood ready to help, starting with a free subscription to our Text2Give fundraising tool to anyone fighting racism and discrimination or working to support impacted communities.

The steps were small moves in the right direction that left me feeling unsatisfied. OneCause exists to bring people together, and we are passionate about inclusivity and building connections. There has never been any place in our organization, or in the future we aim to build, for any kind of prejudice. But it now seemed to me that we had perhaps become too comfortable, complacent even, about simply having an inclusive mission. It wasn't enough to hold the right beliefs. We also had to do the right things. And that meant taking concrete steps to actively and earnestly make our culture more inclusive.

OneCause steers clear of politics. We work with nonprofit organizations of all shapes, sizes, beliefs, and missions, so it's important we remain politically agnostic. But this was different. This wasn't politics. Inequality and injustice were not subjects we could stay silent on. Our Mission is to "Build Better Tomorrows," and there are no better tomorrows that include racism, hate, or prejudice.

During the next five weeks, I returned to this subject three times in my updates, talking about the steps we were taking to become more conscious of bias and more inclusive in our hiring policies. What was harder was sharing how so many of us were feeling. I wanted to write about the sense that our society was experiencing a crisis of confidence, a fraying of the substance that held us together. At the same time, I needed to offer my team a positive vision of the future.

In the end, it felt right to embrace the tension rather than work around it. The honest thing to do was confront these feelings head-on and not allow them to pile on to the extraordinary strains already placed on us by the pandemic. Rather than pass judgment on ourselves, we needed to acknowledge our imperfections and limitations as starting points for a better future.

Memorial Day has always been a day of contrasts—a time to honor and thank those who have made the greatest sacrifice for our nation as well as a time to take a break from work and find pleasure in the company of our families. Memorial Day 2020 will have a legacy of its own for our country. On this day, a man was murdered, five children lost their father, and five siblings lost a brother. On this day, we were all tragically reminded that our society has yet to bury a centuries-long legacy of prejudice, injustice, and racism. But if we move forward together with the goal of overcoming the past, this day might also mark a turning point: the moment we began to change our nation and all our lives for the better.

June 5, 2020

Dear OneCause Nation,

I'd like to begin by reiterating how much I appreciate all of you. I want to continue letting you know that what we all do makes a difference. This week in my update I want to turn my attention away from any stat or success story and reflect on recent events in our nation. For those of you experiencing pain and outrage, I want you to know you are not alone.

We are grappling with some of the most challenging times in our country's history as we face the George Floyd tragedy and the long-term effects of racial injustice while continuing to battle a deadly pandemic. Racism is unacceptable, and we must reject prejudice, injustice, discrimination, and inequality in any form.

At OneCause, we (as a company and employees) have a strong social compass.

Our mission drives us to help build a better tomorrow. These aren't just words about tech, or tools, or fundraising. They are our Why, and they guide all we do.

We work to create good, drive positive impact, and leave the world better than we found it. There's no more important time to continue our stand than now.

We stand firm against the prejudices that pull us apart as a country and as people.

We stand together with all those fighting racial injustice and inequality.

We stand ready to help.

There is much work to be done as a nation, as a company, and as individuals. OneCause is committed to be a part of the change. We have work to do.

You ask, how are we going to do better?

We need to acknowledge that silence is not ok and use our voice.

We need to look at diversity within our own workplace.

We need to address our personal implicit biases.

We need to be open and willing to be educated.

We need to be committed to learning and getting better.

This is a start. Together with our executive management team, we want to be thoughtful in our approach to ensure we create and sustain long-term change.

This effort doesn't come from one team alone or a task force at OneCause. It comes from within all of us. I encourage each of us to reflect on how we can do better as a company.

I realize that each one of you has been impacted by this tragic event in a personal and unique way. Please reach out to me with any ideas and thoughts you have. I want to hear them directly. Now more than ever we need to be united as One Team, OneCause to take action and to help create positive change.

We're sending an email out to our nonprofit customers and reseller partners today, communicating our position and our efforts to help.

Thank you to the many who have come forward to share your thoughts, start a dialogue, and help push us forward.

Together,

Steve

June 19, 2020

Dear OneCause Nation,

It's hard to believe yet another week has gone by, and it's the second half of June already!

While the summer is here, and the weeks fly, we stay focused on our Why—*helping build a better tomorrow and supporting all causes creating positive impact.*

This week marked a huge milestone in our nation's history, with the Supreme Court ruling on key definitions within Title VII of the Civil Rights Act of 1964. This law makes it illegal for an employer to discriminate on the basis of "race, color, religion, sex, or national origin." The ruling this week stated that sexual orientation and gender identity are included in the definition of sex, making it an important and long-awaited victory for LGBTQ+ rights and equality.

As a company, we reject discrimination in any form and support our local LGBTQ+ community and colleagues. We are excited to sponsor and partner in the Indy Pride Virtual Celebration on June 21, 2020. (We had actually planned to participate in the parade last week.) Pride Month is celebrated every June, to pay tribute to the Stonewall riots of 1969, and increase awareness to end discrimination against LGBTQ+ people, while celebrating the community's advancement in achieving fundamental fairness and equality. While there may not be a parade or festival this year, we're excited to be a part of the virtual celebration as a sponsor.

I also want to take a moment to recognize that "Juneteenth" is today. June 19th is recognized as the effective end of slavery in the United States. Although the Emancipation Proclamation went into effect January 1, 1863, it wasn't until June 19, 1865, after the conclusion of the Civil War, that the last of the newly-freed slaves were read President Abraham Lincoln's decree in Texas. The power of this moment in our history takes on added significance in the renewed fight to end racism and discrimination. It's a freedom we hold dear, and I encourage us all to continue to fight for it.

"Hey Steve, how can we do that at OneCause—drive change and not just talk about it?"

We are announcing a new initiative called *OneCause Cares*. OneCause Cares reinforces our strong "Why," focusing on tangible ways to empower our employees to pursue their personal passions and causes, focus on diversity, inclusion, and equality, and create a safe work environment for open dialogue and conversations.

OneCause Cares will also officially bring our mission to life and support initiatives we value as a company. It will help surface new ideas to enhance equality in our workplace and give back to our communities.

Here are a few of the immediate OneCause Cares changes:

- We have rebranded PhilanthroPal to OneCause Cares Days.

- In celebration of Juneteenth, we are adding an extra OneCause Cares day to learn, volunteer, and give back in your communities each year.
- We officially recognize Martin Luther King Jr. Day and Juneteenth as company holidays.
- The YourCause program will be rolled into OneCause Cares.
- OneCause Women in Tech will resume in H2 and be a OneCause Cares initiative.

The executive team will be working together with HR to roll out this program over the summer months. Stay tuned for more information on OneCause Cares at the July Company Meeting. If you are interested in helping us bring OneCause Cares to life, please reach out to me or the HR Team.

You have my commitment to do so for OneCause.

One Team. OneCause. Thank you for all you do.

Steve

July 2, 2020
declara[c]tion.

Happy Independence Day OneCause Nation!

On the 4th of July, we celebrate the adoption of our *Declaration of Independence* from the rule of King George III of Great Britain on July 4, 1776. This was perhaps the most important moment in the history of our nation.

The point of my headline is that this was a **declaration**. A statement. A bold statement, but words nonetheless. In order for those words to have any meaning, they needed to be followed by **action**.

They were, and the result was the formation of the best country in the world! But we clearly have more work to do.

The 4th of July is usually one of my favorites. I've said before that there's no greater sight than the reflection of fireworks in the faces of my children.

But our 4th of July celebration in 2020 is not like the others. We're in the middle of a global pandemic that is currently waging yet another battle through the US—forcing the slowdown and in some cases the shutdown of reopening efforts. There's no 4th of July parade or "Carmelfest" this year. We'll have fireworks, but the mood is different.

We will get through this with relentless positive **action**.

We will look back with wonder.

Our country is also being tested by nationwide calls for justice and equality—the same rights that were promised in the **Declaration** of Independence almost 250 years ago! It's clear that we have a lot more work to do. We need more **action**.

The OneCause mission statement is a **declaration**. It is a statement. It is worthless without **action**. Same with our Values, Vision, and our Why.

We must take **action**. We must live our values. Pursue our Vision with **action** and let those actions be guided by our Why.

So this 4th of July holiday, I ask you to add some *contemplation* to your celebration. We're at the midpoint of 2020. Let's finish strong.

I'm grateful for you for the sacrifices you make every day to take care of our customers and each other. As you spend some time with your loved ones this weekend, please tell them that I am grateful to them too. Every moment you spend pursuing our OneCause mission and vision is time away from them. Thank you.

Make a **declaration**. Follow it with **action**. Help us create a better tomorrow.

Steve

June 19, 2021

pause.

I've been hearing this word a lot.

Last year during the social unrest of the summer, we decided to move with others to recognize Juneteenth by offering an additional day off work. A day to **pause**. To reflect.

Brief History of "Juneteenth"

On June 19, 1865, about two months after the Confederate general Robert E. Lee surrendered at Appomattox, Gordon Granger, a Union general, arrived in Galveston, Texas, to inform enslaved African Americans of their freedom and that the Civil War had ended. General Granger's announcement put into effect the Emancipation

Proclamation, which had been issued more than two and a half years earlier on Jan. 1, 1863, by President Abraham Lincoln.

—The New York Times

This week, Juneteenth was made an official federal holiday. We are very pleased to follow suit and we will make Juneteenth a permanent part of our annual holiday schedule. It is a day to commemorate. It is a day to contemplate. To **pause** and to reflect.

Underrepresented groups in the US have fought for and achieved so much, but *we all have so much more work to do.*

Pause. Reflect. Reimagine. Reengage.

Reflection is empty without action.

FEARLESS FUNDRAISERS IN ACTION
Minneapolis Foundation for Northside Funders Group—Restore North

One bright light in the darkness after George Floyd's death was an incredible fundraising effort by Minneapolis Foundation on behalf of Northside Funders "Restore North" campaign. One of our employees, Dannielle, used her Kickstart Your Cause employee benefit to gift Text2Give to the campaign as it geared up to respond to events in the Twin Cities. To date, Restore North has raised more than $2 million to support Northside business owners who were struggling during an incredibly challenging time for their community.

With pause and reflection and most of all action,

Steve

LEADERSHIP LESSONS

- **Crises are catalysts**
  The appetite for change stirred up by a crisis can be harnessed for broader positive movements. By overturning old certainties and shining new light on old problems, issues, or injustices, a crisis can be a catalyst for a better tomorrow . . . as long as we are willing to accept the challenge.

- **Start a conversation**
  In times of social upheaval, ignoring what's going on in the world beyond the office walls can seem like the easy option. But if you want to build a healthy and inclusive culture, you need to address difficult subjects directly. That means both leading and listening, both talking and creating the time, space, and channels to foster conversation. Big, small, serious, or fun, connecting and talking in times of change binds us together.

- **Live your mission**
  Your mission is your most valuable touchstone when you need to make challenging decisions in a time of crisis. When priorities appear to conflict and you are pulled in multiple directions, focusing on your mission and its underlying values will light the path forward. Your *Why* is more than just words; it is a code to live by.

CHAPTER 5

Innovation Finds a Way

OneCause is a tech company. From the earliest days of the business, our goal has been to leverage advances in software, hardware, and connectivity to support nonprofits in powering their missions. We're always looking for ways to improve our solutions, and we always have at least one eye on our next generation of fundraising products.

When the pandemic hit, we went into crisis-management mode. With fundraising events and revenues flipped off like a light switch quite literally overnight, we needed to streamline processes, manage expenditures, and stabilize the business so it would last the course. Looking at our financials, it was hard not to see a bullseye over the product development budget. When you're trying to work out how to survive the next couple of months, long-term investments with no immediate payoffs become tempting areas to cut. After all, pushing these projects off until after the crisis sounds like an easy win.

It was impossible not to consider the idea. But I didn't take it seriously for a second. Innovation is a key part of the OneCause identity, and curiosity and helpfulness are two of our core values. How could we hold on to who we were as a team if we stopped being curious? How could we look ourselves in the eye if we took the easy route, rather than finding new ways to be helpful?

It just wasn't going to happen. We weren't going to weather the storm by giving up on who we were. Instead, we would be inspired by the challenges, and we would find a way through them to serve the thousands of causes that relied on us.

I was determined that OneCause would come out of this crisis stronger than before. Whenever the stock market crashes, seasoned investors are quick to yell, "Buy the dip!" as they take advantage of the fire sale and expand their positions when everyone else is selling. The same applies to building a business.

By leaning into a crisis and "buying" when everyone else is in retreat, you can often achieve more than when the market is operating under its usual conditions. Sure, we fortified the castle walls and made sure our treasury was protected, but we kept investing in the future because we *knew* that there was a unique opportunity to create value for our nonprofit customers.

Just a few days into the crisis, our chief product officer proposed not only staying the course but throwing everything we had into the development of our next-generation product. I was ready to listen. We were already working on a platform that would change how people saw the future of fundraising. Now, with traditional in-person galas and auctions shut down for the foreseeable future, a solution that could seamlessly connect donors and causes without bringing them physically together had become an immediate necessity. So what became clear in this moment of crisis (and opportunity) was that development of our planned next-generation product would also have to include additional virtual and livestream functionality.

By building on the work we had already done, we could rapidly roll out a solution that met the emerging virtual fundraising need, but only if we were willing to *fully* commit our resources. As an executive team, we didn't need a lot of persuading. The only condition I set was that the new product had to fulfill its original purpose. We were building the future of our fundraising platform. It couldn't just be thrown together at speed to meet immediate needs; it had to work in the long term as well.

Despite being pulled from their regular work environments and forced to adapt to working from spare bedrooms or kitchen tables, the development team had a pilot version up and running in just three months. By the fall fundraising season, the new virtual and livestream fundraising solution was ready to go.

The new product would enable an auctioneer in Kentucky and someone in Florida to cast a bid while an audience around the country watched the action live. A nonprofit could pair co-hosts in different locations and cut from one to the other in real time, putting together a professional-quality stream with a simple and intuitive editing suite. This new product shifted the dial on what was possible across the industry.

The team's ability to deliver on time while staying laser focused on optimizing the system to meet rapidly evolving customer needs was awe-inspiring. Every time they ran into a challenge, they found a way around it, through it, or over it. They were unstoppable. Watching them work made me proud to be part of the OneCause Nation.

I was so excited by what was going on behind the scenes that it was hard not to make the new platform's progress a regular feature of my weekly updates. Two things held me back. In the early weeks and months, I couldn't yet be sure that the new solution would be delivered on schedule, so it was important not to make grand announcements until we were certain.

In addition, I didn't want to compromise the personal dimension of the message that kicked off each update. I was determined to use that space to connect, provide support, and share tools and ways of thinking I had found personally useful. Instead of discussing our business strategy and product plans, my excitement inspired me to write about the importance of a vision for the future and the value of embracing change.

As the new platform progressed, it took on a deeper meaning for me. It was always more than just a tech project, but increasingly it became a symbol of how we were going to get through the pandemic. It was a nugget of hope, a glimpse of the lotus emerging from the muck, not just in spite of what we were enduring, but *because* of it.

In the second week of June, I shared that we had reached an important milestone: the first "mock" event executed on the new platform. I was staggered by how far we had come in such a short time—the achievement felt monumental.

Two weeks later, I was thinking about how another business, Live Nation, had approached the crisis and found a way to deliver their own product—live music events—despite the COVID restrictions. The parallels with our own achievement were too striking to ignore.

So for the first and only time in 2020, I used my message at the start of the update to talk about our new product and how we could use it to do more for the nonprofits we worked with. It had to come out. It meant so much that I couldn't keep being open and honest without writing about it.

As we moved through the year, I continued to trickle out information on the progress of our new fundraising platform in the "business" section of the weekly updates. But my personal messages steered clear of the topic . . . with one exception.

Just before Christmas, an event of global, historical importance took place: a 90-year-old British woman, Margaret Keenan, became the first person to receive the fully-tested Pfizer vaccine. I couldn't resist drawing a parallel once again. Like OneCause, humanity and innovation had found a way.

April 30, 2020

a bit of certainty in a world of uncertainty.

In a world of uncertainty, we humans crave certainty. (Paradoxically in a world of certainty, we'll tend to crave uncertainty, but let's stick with the first premise for now. We're fickle creatures. ☺)

In my "many" years on this planet, I don't remember a time of more uncertainty.

So, I'd like to offer you some *certainty* today.

We will (again):

- Shake hands (despite what some may say).
- Send our kids back to school.
- Greet someone with a hug.
- Go to a movie.
- Go on a date.
- Go to church.
- Go out to dinner.
- Enjoy a live concert.
- Trust.
- Believe.
- Touch a doorknob without fear.
- Get a haircut.
- Work in the office.
- Go to a ballgame.
- Travel.
- *Attend a fundraising gala.*

The list goes on. Make your own list of the things you long for. We will do those things again. But we also know that it won't all happen at once, and we may not necessarily go back to *exactly* the way things were. In fact, we may go back to better. The key is that you have to establish the right timeline for your vision. We WILL do all of these things. We WON'T do all these things next week or next month.

We're starting to see small movements toward getting back to "normal." Cities and states are beginning to lift their "stay-at-home/ shelter-in-place" directives. The key will be incremental steps of progress toward the outcome we envision.

Create your Vision. Make your Plan. Find your Why. Get it done.

OneCause has a vision for fundraising that has not changed. We DO have a *new plan*. We're still driven by our Why. We're getting it done. We will get back to all the things we long for. Set your sights on that vision for the future and then focus on our day-to-day execution. A few small wins every day. George Washington supposedly liked to say, *"Many mickles make a muckle."* Well said, George!

We're starting to string a few "mickles" of our own together . . .

This week the product team unveiled code-name "Marauder"— our new fundraising solution featuring **video streaming** (live and pre-recorded), donations, raffles, donor engagement, sponsorship opportunities, and more! This was a first look into our vision for the future of "virtual" on our new fundraising platform. Marauder was a whiteboard drawing just four weeks ago! Great teamwork product and engineering!

FEARLESS FUNDRAISING IN ACTION
All in for Fiver—Stay at Home Benefit

All in for Fiver—Stay at Home Benefit was a great success this Tuesday—bringing together the community virtually to celebrate 20 years of the Fiver Children's Foundation and their work with youth and families in New York City and Central New York that continues through these challenging times. The organization created an elaborate event website using text messaging, pre-recorded videos, and interactive "virtual rooms" (cocktail lounge, photobooth, and after party) to keep their supporters engaged. The team was thrilled with the shift to the virtual event and continues to reach their fundraising goals.

QUOTE OF THE WEEK

"We had to take our event virtual. We knew we had no choice. We had donors say they felt this event was more impactful and personal, because we were able to call out names of real time donations coming in. It gave people extra fulfillment and we think helped bring in more donations."

—Michael, Development Director, Tennessee Kidney Foundation

We need to take this result and multiply it by ten. But, as I said earlier, we need to notch a few small wins every day on the way to the outcome we envision.

So, another week has come and gone. In the past few weeks, we've started to see some positive momentum in bookings, event conversions, and customer and prospect engagement. Positive progress. One step at a time.

I appreciate everything you do.

Keep fighting!

Steve

June 11, 2020

"Ch-Ch-Ch-Ch-Changes"

—David Bowie

I was trying to put my finger on the feeling I was having yesterday. The decision to move out of our offices at the end of this month creates a massive logistical puzzle that needs to be solved in a fairly short period of time, but I was energized, not overwhelmed. Rick and his team are handling it with calm and professionalism. No worries.

The office itself is filled with good memories of company growth and success. I was also unearthing presentations and notebooks from the old BidPal days that reminded me that we train ourselves to mostly remember the good things. ☺ There were also some very tough times. But we got through them—together.

With all the events in our world, there is uncertainty ahead that we must navigate.

What I was feeling was the mixed emotions that come with **"change."**

We're experiencing change at an exponential rate. We're generally not suited for this.

My Calm app came through again . . .

"Life changes . . . we can wake up in the morning in a world unrecognizable from yesterday . . . the path that we've so carefully chosen takes us in a new and uncertain direction . . . fighting change is futile . . . rather than struggling for control . . . loosen our grip . . . let go . . . and get comfortable with uncertainty . . . flow with the current rather than fighting it . . . get more comfortable riding the waves of change."

"There is nothing so stable as change."

—Bob Dylan

Let's get comfortable with uncertainty. Don't fight it. Flow with it. Make it work for us.

This helps me to think in this way. I hope it helps you too.

And finally—wow, just wow!

Like you, I just witnessed the historical first "mock event" featuring our Virtual Fundraising Solution and benefiting Second Helpings. There are so many people who worked so hard to make this happen. To begin to list all their names would 100% ensure that I would forget someone, so I will just say a HUGE THANKS TO EVERYONE who made this happen. The future is very bright indeed!

So, here's to change! Embrace it. Flow with it. Make it work for you!

Riding the waves of change,

Steve

June 26, 2020

find a way.

This week's inspiration comes from an unlikely source—as inspiration often does. Sue and I just booked our "ticket" to see Brad Paisley live at the Ruoff Music Center (formerly known as "Klipsch," among other names), the outdoor music venue in Noblesville, IN. Most of you know that I love music. I particularly love live music.

I miss live music.

I miss live music performed outdoors under the stars on a hot Midwestern summer night.

Brad Paisley and his band miss the road, the crowds, and the revenue.

Live Nation (promoter and venue owner) misses the revenue.

They needed to **find a way**. Introducing—"The Live Nation Live from the Drive-In Tour."

Created as a way to reimagine the live music experience during a time of social distancing, the Live From The Drive-In concert series enables you to enjoy concerts from your own individual tailgating zone.

They've turned the outdoor concert inside out. The stage is set up on the parking lot and "tickets" are sold per car with a dedicated area for viewing the show, having a picnic + appropriate social distancing space.

Brad Paisley wins.

Live Nation wins.

We win.

It's not going to be perfect, but they **found a way**.

Sound familiar to you? It should.

This is what we are all doing every day. We're finding a way for our *customers* to keep fundraising. We're finding a way for our *prospects* to engage with OneCause for the first time and fundraise with us. We're being passionate, curious, helpful, and committed to **finding a way** to be a trusted guide to virtual, online, text-based, and peer-to-peer fundraising solutions while our customers wait to gather again back in the ballroom. We can't wait, and we have to get them to take action too.

Soon, we will be offering the Virtual Fundraising Solution as the next iteration of "**finding a way**" to fundraise.

I went looking for a good quote and found this one attributed to Confucius himself (or entrepreneur Jim Rohn, depending on who you ask!):

> *"One who wants to do something will find a way.*
> *One who doesn't will find an excuse."*
>
> *—Confucius*

We're not about excuses. We must be bold, be creative, and think different(ly).

So, I encourage you to keep doing what you're doing, but if you feel bogged down, stay committed and—**find a way**.

I'd love it if you dropped me a note/reply to this email with an example of how you or one of your customers have found a new way to help our fearless fundraisers be bold, creative, and successful!

No excuses. Find a way.

Steve

September 5, 2020

patience.

"The two most powerful warriors are patience and time."

—Leo Tolstoy

We are not a patient society. I was going through a promo video with Karrie the other day for Raise. It was at 1:46 (one minute and 46 seconds) and I was like, "OK, this is getting long."

We send a text—we immediately want to see the reply "bubbles" to indicate that the recipient is working on a response.

I "do not like" going to the grocery store. (I was brought up to not say the word "hate.") This was the same pre-COVID. I am impatient—with other people, with finding stuff, and with standing in line. I do not like standing in line.

We're finding our patience tested like never before. When is this going to be over? When will we be back to normal? When can my kids go back to school? When will we be able to shake hands or greet each other with a hug?

No one knows. Be patient.

But like a predator with prey, patience can also be a great weapon. Synonyms include perseverance, tenacity, and endurance.

This is the patience of battle. This is the patience needed for victory.

We're in a battle right now, and we need to show patience.

Be patient with our customers. They are confused and maybe even scared. They need our help.

Be patient with your family. Your kids. Your spouse. Your partner. We're all a little annoyed.

Be patient with your OneCause teammates. Everyone reacts differently to stress. We can't know what others are dealing with. We need each other to succeed.

Be patient with the world. Even with the grocery store. ☺

We've been watching some of the US Open tennis. For those of you who play tennis, you know that you have to be patient at the baseline in order to set up the "winner." Baseball players have to show patience at the plate to get a "pitch to hit."

Then they need to strike with quickness, strength, and fluidity.

Patience will put us in position to win.

We will win.

Also wanted to update you on something really exciting:

Virtual Fundraising Solution

This past week marked the most exciting moment for OneCause in the "COVID Era." We announced the release and immediate availability of the OneCause Virtual Fundraising Solution!

The new fundraising software represents the product of a year and a half of development and readiness planning squeezed into the past five months since mid-March. So much of OneCause Nation was involved in this process that I won't try to recognize anyone individually. Such amazing work from an amazing team!

With patience,

Steve

December 14, 2020

Who is Margaret Keenan?

"I'll take *Moments in COVID history for $600, Chance.*"

It's 2040. Chance "the Rapper" is now just "Chance." He's always been way more than "the Rapper." He's a philanthropist, advocate for justice and equity, Sox fan, and now the host of Jeopardy!

Chance—*"This 90-year-old grandmother of four made history on December 8, 2020, as the first recipient of the Pfizer COVID vaccine."*

Contestant—*"Who is Margaret Keenan."*

Chance—*"Correct!"* ☺

My weekly update this week is a little tardy but comes with the good news that history has been made. Last week, on Tuesday, December 8th, the first "needle in the arm" containing a COVID vaccine from Pfizer was delivered to Margaret "Maggie" Keenan in the United Kingdom.

Today, Monday December 14th, NYC nurse Sandra Lindsay was among the first to receive the vaccination in the US.

Let's take a moment and *live* in history being made.

It was a "shot heard round the world."

This was not Ralph Waldo Emerson's tale of the first shot taken by American Patriots at the battle of Lexington and Concord. Nor was it the New York [baseball] Giants' Bobby Thomson's game-winning homerun against the Brooklyn Dodgers in 1951 to win the National League pennant. No, even I was not alive for that one. Haha! ☺

This "shot heard round the world" is our first *counterattack* in our ongoing *battle* against the Coronavirus and its disease COVID.

Good vs. Bad

Darkness vs. Light

The Rebel Alliance vs. the Galactic Empire

With news of second and third surges and escalating hospital-izations, cases, and deaths, it couldn't have come at a better time.

cautious optimism.

Mark and I presented our proposed budget for 2021 last week and it was approved by the Board.

If there is one spot-on expression for this plan for next year it is "cautious optimism."

The first part of the year we will be taking a cautious approach. We're optimistic about the future, but still pragmatic about our current situation. Spring '21 will likely look a lot like Fall '20.

We're optimistic about the second half of 2021! With the contin-ued maturity and development of the Virtual Fundraising Solution into the full Fundraising Platform with integration with Peer-to-Peer, we will fulfill our vision as set forth in 2017!

With pent-up demand and renewed optimism, there may be a massive surge in event fundraising. Face-to-face fundraising will return (albeit with a virtual component) in the fall of 2021. This is the rise of hybrid.

I'm feeling it!

There is light at the end of the tunnel. We're leading and advancing toward it!

With hope,

Steve

LEADERSHIP LESSONS

- **Harness a service mindset**
  The passionate desire to serve others provides a springboard for creative change. A commitment to helping causes that really matter gives meaning to our work and motivates our quest for solutions.

- **Uncertainty can be a positive**
  Chaos, change, and uncertainty are engines of innovation. The overturning of established orders and the need to respond to the unexpected force us to find new ways to achieve our goals. As scary as it can be, use the hole created by upheaval to chart a new course or embrace a "silver-lining" mindset.

- **Build a culture of curiosity**
  The ability to embrace change and find opportunities in chaos is rooted in culture. These conditions can only give rise to innovation if people and the organizations to which they belong embrace them. Fear of change leads to a retreat into what is familiar and safe, so a culture of curiosity and fearlessness is necessary to make the most of upheavals when they arrive.

CHAPTER 6

Decision Points

By the end of July 2020, we had been working from home for four months. Thanks to the incredible OneCause IT team, the transition had been almost seamless. Our entire organization was operating remotely, using digital tools to keep in touch and run distributed home offices in a way we could only have imagined a year earlier.

Yet no matter how effective our virtual infrastructure was, there were some things it couldn't replace: the experience of working a few feet away from like-minded people in pursuit of a shared mission, the opportunity to grab a coffee with friends, the stories and jokes told over cubicles. While we could all communicate using online tools, there was no easy replacement for the physical presence that anchored us to each other throughout the day.

These changes affected everyone, but we weren't all impacted in the same way or to the same degree. With my kids grown and out of the house, I could work from the kitchen table in my home in Carmel in relative peace. It wasn't easy to be away from the team, but it wasn't hard to work in the space and time available to me.

For other team members, the situation was very different. Many OneCausers were working out of basements or bedrooms. Some were sharing desks with their partners while others were dialing into meetings from the couch because they didn't have a spare table to use.

More than one team member turned a closet into a makeshift office so they could have doors that closed to give them a little privacy. The need to create new workspaces upended homes and introduced new tensions and stresses into everyday life.

The many OneCausers who were parents of school-age children had even more balls to keep in the air. I miss my kids every day now that they're adults. One of the greatest pains of the early months of the pandemic was not being able to see them in person. I wanted to hug them, be near them, and to share the physical closeness that's so basic to family life. But the idea of bringing that closeness into my work environment—all day, every day, for months at a time—while homeschooling, monitoring screen time, and generally stopping them from going stir crazy . . . it was hard to even imagine.

Throughout the company, people were hurting, and I needed to acknowledge that difficult reality in my updates. I wanted to offer something more than platitudes, something practical and useful, but I knew that any advice would have to come from a place of humility. I couldn't solve everyone's problems, and any attempt to do so would have been tone-deaf. But what I could do was invite everyone to give themselves something truly precious: the gift of time.

I started reading business books and articles in my late 20s, looking for insights that could help me develop in my career. I wanted to know what was going on in the economy and how companies were structured. I was curious about how to grow sales, manage capital, and build teams, cooperate with colleagues, provide leadership, and take instruction.

Interestingly, the more I read, the less comfortable I became with the idea that there was some separate world of "business management" at all. Insights about "workers," "teams," "management," and "leadership" were really just ways of thinking about how humans behave as individuals and as groups. Ultimately, I realized that there was little in the business literature that couldn't be applied in the wider world as well.

Music, art, science, spirituality, family, warfare—in fact, any field of human activity or reflection—can provide inspiration for the way we live our lives. But one of the great things about business and organizational tools is that they tend to be practical and results-oriented. So I decided to use my July 31st update to share a tool introduced to me early in my career.

I came across it in Stephen Covey's world renowned book *The 7 Habits of Highly Effective People*, but it was on my mind again because I had recently read about Covey's own inspiration: Eisenhower's Decision Matrix. This simple framework provides a method for streamlining time management using the categories of "important" and "urgent" to prioritize activities.

In particular, it shines a spotlight on activities that aren't important at all, encouraging us to cut out the things in our lives that are non-essential (see Chapter 3). When we take this approach, we are rewarded with extra time for things that really matter. This, I hoped, had the potential to be a lifeline for busy parents in particular.

Another dimension of the Eisenhower Matrix had special value in the context of the pandemic: it doesn't just draw attention to the important things that need to be done right now. The Eisenhower Matrix identifies the equally important things that have been sitting on the sidelines because they aren't urgent.

In doing so, it encourages us to invest in ourselves by recognizing the importance of that language course, sales seminar, or IT certification we have been putting off. It also reminds us that, if we are to thrive in the long term, we need to invest time in our social relationships. Just as the pandemic had disrupted the boundaries between home and work, it had also thrown up new barriers between the individual and the group.

In a world of "social distancing," it's more important than ever to reach out and reforge the bonds that sustain us through the hard times.

July 31, 2020

urgent and important.

This week I was doing some reading and came across a reference to the "Eisenhower Matrix." Upon further review, the discussion was around the balance and prioritization of what is "urgent" and what is "important." Being a product of the '80s business generation, I said, "Hey, that's Stephen Covey. Not Eisenhower. That's from the *Seven Habits of Highly Effective People*." It might actually be the only thing I remembered from it. ☺

Well, apparently Stephen Covey **popularized** this notion of classifying our actions into a matrix of urgency and importance, but its origin is attributed to Dwight D. Eisenhower. We all recognize his name from history class, but *what did this guy really do*? (from the Web):

- **Five-star** general in the US Army who crafted the strategy for the Allied invasion of Europe
- Two-term US President responsible for:
    - The construction of the US Interstate System
    - The creation of NASA
    - First major piece of civil rights legislation since the end of the Civil War
    - Ended the Korean War
    - Welcomed Hawaii and Alaska as states
    - Managed the beginnings of the US/Soviet Cold War

What have you done, Steve? Well, not that. So this guy probably knows a little bit about time management and prioritization.

As we now complete 4 ½ months of disruption to our lives due to the Coronavirus and its disease COVID, we continue to seek new strategies for balancing our daily demands.

I want to specifically call out and recognize the OneCause parents of school-aged kids facing the uncertainty of the fall classroom. Will it be attended? Virtual? Hybrid? Whatever decision is made, there's the proven and constant uncertainty that things can change in the blink of an eye with a sudden surge in new cases or if a teacher or child tests positive in your school.

To say that "*I know how you feel*" would be inaccurate. I can imagine it, but my kids are grown.

So, I will say that I and your leadership know that you are facing (yet again) unprecedented disruption to your lives and the lives of your kids. We will get through this new challenge, and we will do it together with you with grace and understanding.

Perhaps you can derive some inspiration from this short piece of "balance" provided by Eisenhower and Covey.

The Urgent and Important Matrix:

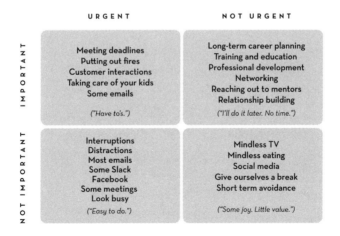

	URGENT	NOT URGENT
IMPORTANT	Meeting deadlines Putting out fires Customer interactions Taking care of your kids Some emails *("Have to's.")*	Long-term career planning Training and education Professional development Networking Reaching out to mentors Relationship building *("I'll do it later. No time.")*
NOT IMPORTANT	Interruptions Distractions Most emails Some Slack Facebook Some meetings Look busy *("Easy to do.")*	Mindless TV Mindless eating Social media Give ourselves a break Short term avoidance *("Some joy. Little value.")*

Then what Eisenhower does is to give us an action overlay:

The Eisenhower Decision Matrix

	URGENT	NOT URGENT
IMPORTANT	**Do** Do it now.	**Decide** Schedule a time to do it.
NOT IMPORTANT	**Delegate** Who can do it for you?	**Delete** Eliminate it.

- **Urgent and Important**—You just have to do it.
- **Not Urgent but Important**—Find the time to do it. Make it a priority. Invest in your future self.
- **Urgent but Not Important**—Find another way. Delegate. Control.
- **Not Urgent and Not Important**—Stop doing it. Limit it. Finally, eliminate it.

You have challenges and demands on your time today. In a couple of weeks, there's going to be a new dynamic to that challenge:

Back to School.

I hope you can use this tool to help with your daily, weekly, monthly, or periodic planning and prioritization sessions. This is really just an introduction to the concept, so I'd encourage you to do some deeper research if you are interested.

FEARLESS FUNDRAISING IN ACTION

Kidsave International—Virtual National Miracles Gala 2020

Kidsave replaced their annual gala with the Virtual National Miracles Gala so they could keep fundraising for the cause. On their Giving Center, they included: an online auction, registration through ticketing to receive a link to the livestream, and a donation tab. (They are keeping their donation tab open until July 31st!) On the night of their virtual event, more than 1,000 supporters came together to drive exciting fundraising. And still hopefully more to come online.

QUOTE OF THE WEEK

"If you can make it easy to donate and make your mission very clear as to where donors' funds are going, virtual fundraising is a home run."

—Terri, Director of Special Events, Boys & Girls Club of Greater Washington

WOW! Thank you, Terri! Sometimes it just has to be said. Make it easy to donate. Make your mission clear and communicate the impact that donors' funds are making. Does anyone remember EMI from our research? Ease. Mission. Impact. Nailed it.

Notice that Customer Success story? This was a historical week for the Virtual Fundraising Solution: our first pilot. Congratulations again to all the teams involved for not only getting us ready for our all-company mock event last week (I couldn't resist that Pete Rose autographed baseball!!) but also for executing our first pilot event! Take a moment to celebrate!

So, as you get ready to go "Back to School," we all know that we have to do the Urgent and Important stuff. I encourage you to schedule just 10% more time to do the Important but Not Urgent stuff that is an investment in your future. It's easy to put off. It's easy to convince yourself that you just don't have the time. You may not see immediate yield, but it will be worth it. Put the TV remote down and spend more time with your kids, plan your summer 2021 vacation (the one you didn't get to take this year), call someone you have been thinking about, and learn more about our country's leaders.

Keep on climbing,

Steve

August 7, 2020

Congratulations OneCause Nation!

Simply by clicking on this email, you have given yourself the opportunity to have your **Best. Week. Ever.**

As the sweepstakes say, "*you may have already won!*" Look inside for details.

From time to time in my weekly updates, I've quoted from what have been referred to as "the Stoics." My first experience with the Stoics was Marcus Aurelius' *Meditations*. Author Ryan Holiday brings the ancient writings of Seneca, Marcus Aurelius, and others forward into our modern-day world. They are remarkably fitting.

I have also thought of them as "common sense." But the tricky thing about common sense is—so many people don't apply it. We're too busy. We're distracted. We don't have enough time. We know better.

I came across this *posting* from Ryan Holiday and was immediately inspired to share it with you as this week's message. It was so common sense. So logical. Yet, so insightful, and inspiring.

If you truly apply this approach to your daily life, you will indeed create your best day/week/month/quarter/year ever.

Here are the highlights (7 steps) as originally presented by Ryan Holiday, followed by some observations from me:

1. Rise and Shine
    a. Let's go! Get yourself out of bed. No snooze button. Get up 15 minutes earlier each week until you're getting up an hour earlier. This is my advice. I need to follow my own advice, Just Do It.
    b. Also, don't waste your morning brain working out. Get out your journal. Plan your day. Send some emails.
    c. Now that you're WFH, work out later after you've cranked out some work.
2. Prepare Yourself for Negativity
    a. What does he mean by that? I don't want you to be jaded. Just be prepared. Don't be surprised by stupid $%^& that happens. Know that it's going to and be ready for it.
    b. If we aren't thinking this way, we'll feel things like, "Life isn't fair," or think, "Why does this just happen to me?" Guess what? It doesn't just happen to you. It happens to all of us. Be ready for it.

3. Clarify Your Principles

    a. This is like your own personal OneCause Values. What do you stand for? What won't you stand for from others?

    b. The great Hoosier John Cougar Mellenkamp once sang, *"You gotta stand for something or you'll fall for anything."*

    c. Open a Word doc and type at the top: "I believe . . ." and then let your words flow. Your brain will work much faster than you can type. You'll have ten things listed immediately. I do this every few years. It changes. You change.

4. Be Ruthless to the Things That *Don't Matter*

    a. I've already written a little about this in my—"Dead" vs. "Alive" time update.

    b. This particular piece gave some good guidance on the use of the word "no." Learn to say it. I have trouble with this, because I consider "helping people" to be a guiding principle. So, I have to say "no" to other things so that I can make time for saying "yes" to helping people.

5. Turn "Have to" into "Get to"

    a. This requires some discipline. It's easy to wallow in self-pity and say, "I have to" finish this report, make this call, do this research, wear this mask, social distance, etc.

    b. I loved this quote attributed to Marcus A., ". . . *this is fortunate that it happened to me*" because not everyone would have been able to handle it.

    c. I get to serve as the CEO of OneCause! I get to help lead this company through the biggest setback most of us have ever experienced in our personal and professional lives. I get to work with some of the best people on the planet. I get to help thousands of nonprofits raise hundreds of millions of dollars for their causes. I get to help fix the world.

6. Take a Walk (or a Run)

    a. With WFH, this feels like it should be easier to do. However, WFH also entails taking care of kids, home schooling, and other distractions. So, it might be just as difficult.

    b. Schedule the time. Set it aside on your calendar and do it.

    c. I know that I am usually all about music. For this purpose, leave the music behind. Find quiet time to think.

    d. In order to have a creative breakthrough, you need to quiet your mind. That's why we think of some of our greatest ideas in the shower!

    e. Take a walk.

7. Review

    a. This is the perfect end to the day because it sets you up for Step 1—Rise and Shine! A virtuous circle.

    b. If you **review** the day you just had and make a compelling plan for tomorrow, you set yourself up for success. What did you do well? What did you learn? What value did you create?

    c. This quote from Winston Churchill is great: *"Every night I try myself by Court Martial to see if I have done anything effective during the day. I don't mean just pawing the ground, anyone can go through the motions, but something really effective."* We don't have to put ourselves on trial every night like dear Winston, but we should hold ourselves to a high standard like doing "something really effective."

    d.   If you feel like you didn't do that today, make a plan for a better tomorrow.

OK, you now have the Secret to Success—just by opening this email. No purchase required!
Lather. Rinse. Repeat.

Let me know what happens!

Steve

August 16, 2020
friendship.

I'm starting my weekly update at the end of the dock on a picturesque western Michigan lake. We're visiting good friends who we have not seen since *the day the earth stood still* in mid-March.

It's barely noon, but the lake is buzzing. Pontoons, speedboats, water-skiers, kayaks, and wave-runners create an ever-moving landscape of sights and sounds. Despite the cacophony of the activity on the lake, I sit calm. Almost serene. Life has been unbelievably challenging, but we have all risen to that challenge, and we're still "OK."

I'm thinking about friendships. I'm thinking about my update from a couple of weeks ago where I touched on the intersection of "Urgent" and "Important." Friendship falls in the category of Not Urgent, but Important.

That's the category we need to work on for our continued development and to have a fulfilling life.

Unfortunately, though, friendships are one of the things that we tend to let go of and also take for granted. In times of crisis, you focus on the primary need of your immediate family. You focus on the priorities of your work and making a living—to provide for your family. It's understandable and OK.

As we move from disaster response to recovery, I'd like to encourage you to take the time to rekindle friendships you may have put off.

Most friendships can survive a long time without care and feeding. I know what you're thinking. We all have those friends from college that we can reconnect with, and very soon it's as if we never were out of touch. But don't take that for granted.

It turns out that friendship is good for your soul AND your body. A Harvard study of men across their lives from 20 to 80 found that the single best predictor of our health and happiness at 80 was not your wealth or your professional success. It was your relationships at age 50.

So, make a list. At the top, two columns: Personal and Professional. We have professional friendships that need to be cultivated too! List the names of five personal and professional friends you'd like to reconnect with and send emails out right now.

Remember, email first. Don't just pick up the phone—particularly if you've been out of touch.

It's not the '70s anymore. People don't just call. That's "just weird," as my kids say.

There's a protocol.

Reconnect virtually today but make plans for getting together to share a meal, coffee, or a happy hour when that is all possible again. You'll be surprised at how much pleasure just making the list gives you—let alone actually reaching out!

Do it! ☺

FEARLESS FUNDRAISING IN ACTION
YWCA of Oklahoma City—2020 Purple Sash Gala

This past Friday, we operated our first in-venue full-service event since COVID hit with the YWCA of Oklahoma City's 2020 Purple Sash Gala. While the event may have looked different as onsite guests were provided with sponsor-donated masks, the YWCA was still able to provide a fun, safe cocktail evening experience while raising money for their important domestic violence programs. Onsite guests enjoyed hors d'oeuvres, a live auction, and a silent auction. Additionally, virtual guests were invited to participate in the silent auction for the first-time ever, with updates provided on social media.

QUOTE OF THE WEEK

This week's Quote of the Week comes to us from a stellar G2 Crowd Review—

*"Our nonprofit Zoo was closed to the public for almost three months, due to the pandemic. During that time, we raised critical funds through OneCause's mobile bidding software. The ease of creating auctions and the extensive detail they put into creating the peer-to-peer software are second to none. **OneCause is hands-down the***

best fundraising software our nonprofit has ever utilized, with not only competitive pricing but exceptional features and customer service. Our organization navigated both the peer-to-peer fundraising software and the mobile bidding software with ease [...] We highly recommend using OneCause and are elated with our experiences with them this year."

Have a great week.

Onward!

Steve

LEADERSHIP LESSONS

- **Distinguish the urgent from the important**
  Not everything important is urgent and not everything that seems urgent is important. Taking a moment to distinguish between the two can cut your stress levels dramatically. Leading, modeling, and sharing this simple philosophy with your team can help everyone stay calm, aligned, and directionally focused on the right, most impactful things.

- **Eliminate the non-essential**
  If something is neither urgent nor important, you can let it go completely. Give yourself the gift of time by cutting out anything that's not essential.

- **Go back to basics**

  When the world is upside down and nothing seems to make sense, fall back on what you know works. Use simple proven tools for business that can help make sense of other parts of life as well. Believe it or not, going back to basics can have a radical impact.

- **Invest in yourself**

  Identifying things in our lives that are important but not urgent helps remind us not to let opportunities for growth slip by. Setting aside a portion of time specifically for non-urgent but important things ensures we create the space to develop ourselves and our careers, or even just reconnect with people, activities, or interests we've let slip by. Stop and focus outside of the moment.

CHAPTER 7

Who We Are (Part I)
Passionate and Curious

Traditionally, fall marks the beginning of the end of the annual cycle. The sun starts to dip a little earlier every day, the nights lengthen, the weather turns cold, and the wind starts shaking the leaves from the trees. Where spring symbolizes new beginnings, fall is about the harvest, and nestling in around the fireplace to prepare for the winter that lies ahead.

Traditionally . . .

For OneCause, fall is always an important and busy time of year, a key fundraising period that is critical for many of the nonprofits we serve. But with 2020 upending expectations on all fronts, fall became something more for us. It was almost like a second spring, a replacement for the months lost earlier in the year. With lockdowns easing and the rollout of our new Virtual Fundraising Solution, it felt like a fresh start, a season of renewal. The pandemic was far from over, and we knew well enough by now how fast things could change. But as a business, the year's first blossoms were starting to show.

In September, we held Raise 2020, our annual nonprofit fundraising conference. It was the largest yet, with more than 7,000 fearless fundraisers from 43 countries around the world. We even had people checking in from the Amazon Rainforest!

Two weeks later, the OneCause executive management team sat down to do some blue-sky thinking about our future. Not satisfied with looking a few months or years ahead, we tried to imagine where OneCause would be in 10 years' time. It was a challenging exercise, especially in the middle of a pandemic that was overturning so much that we thought was certain.

To help us think about how we might evolve, we spent time reflecting on where we were now. We looked at our trajectory over the last few years, and we talked a lot about our company values and how they shaped our expectations for the future.

Two weeks later, those values were still on my mind. Thinking about the future and watching the burst of activity blown in by the fall winds reminded me just how important our collective identity was to everything we do.

OneCause Values have evolved since I joined the company. When I first came on board, the business was in the middle of a big shift. We were moving from the explosive growth of the startup phase to the goal of scaling the company in a sustainable way to build an enduring presence in the fundraising landscape. That transition came with a particular set of challenges, and our values at the time were shaped to meet them. Those values aimed to help us move across that threshold to sustainable growth. But once we were there, our needs changed.

What it meant to be part of the OneCause Nation became something different, so we embarked on a journey to create a new set of values. These were chosen not only because they defined what we had become, but because they provided a framework to support our actions and decision making as we moved forward.

Those values continue today to reflect who we are and who we want to be, holding us together as one team with one cause: to empower our fearless fundraisers and their missions.

As we moved into October, I decided to devote a series of four updates to our core values. I had referenced them in passing throughout the year, but with new activity emerging, new technologies coming into play, and innovation creating momentum for us, it seemed like the right time to remind everyone of the culture we shared. Writing about our values was a way to keep us connected in spirit at a time when we were all physically apart.

Our OneCause four values are set in a specific order because they build on each other. The relationship between the first two is particularly powerful.

Our first value is "We are passionate." Passion is the fuel that drives us forward, it's the gas in the tank that keeps us energized and engaged, even when we're tired, even when fundraising events in the world around us are creating pressures and strains we never expected to face.

We're fortunate that it is so easy to be passionate about the nonprofits we work with. Every single day we support incredible causes, helping other passionate people raise money to build better tomorrows. It's not hard to be inspired!

The passion that drives us connects naturally with our second value: "We are curious." Our curiosity, our desire to understand why something matters or how we can do more, reinforces the passion that gives our work meaning. At the same time, it pushes us to "find a way" (see Chapter 5) through difficulties, to ask why something works or how we can better serve our customers.

That curiosity and wonder at what is possible were central to the work of the product development team in creating the new Virtual Fundraising Solution, but just as important, it was foundational to our sense of community. Curiosity doesn't just drive innovation; it helps foster empathy and personal connections by helping us work to understand each other.

Of all the updates I wrote, the four on our values were perhaps the easiest. Of course, it helped to have a structure mapped out and to know where I was going with each one. But the conscious re-engaging with what defined us as a company was exciting to me. I was passionate about who we were. I was curious about what we could achieve together. And as I sat at my kitchen table halfway through October, I was excited at the opportunity to write about a set of values that had become so deeply ingrained in my own identity.

October 9, 2020

we are passionate.

"Hey there! Remember me? I'm your first value!"

We are passionate.

We are curious.

We are helpful.

We are committed.

When we were formulating and rolling out the values, I was well known for saying, *"These values have to be more than just a nice poster, t-shirt, or coffee mug."* We have to live them. Build them into everything we do from recruiting and hiring to serving our customers, working with each other, and making personnel decisions.

Now that we're all working from home, we don't even have the benefit of seeing a poster in the kitchen, using our values coffee mug during our team meeting, or sporting the OneCause hoodie with the values etched across the back.

We need to do more. We need to continue to reinforce our values. Now more than ever.

So, I thought my weekly update would provide a good forum for doing a deeper dive into each of our four core values—starting with "We are passionate."

First, it was brought to my attention during our recent EMT strategic planning session that each value as stated is and should be accompanied by an *action statement*. Here is the full representation of the first value:

"We are **passionate**."

We strive to make a difference. The passion at OneCause is infectious. We love what we do and are inspired by the customers we work with every day. It's our passion for nonprofits and their missions that drives us to build a better tomorrow.

There are many interpretations and much written around the notion of being passionate. This quote from Oprah reflects for me what I think being passionate means for us as OneCausers.

> *"Passion is energy. Feel the power of focusing on what excites you."*
> Oprah Winfrey

It's not *just* about being passionate but taking that passion and *turning it into the energy* (remember "recharge" from last week?). You need to focus on what excites you and take that next action. Our action statement calls out our "nonprofits and their missions" as our purpose for our passion.

I've also seen this statement. It's not attributed as a quote from anyone. It's not just, "Be passionate." It's remember your purpose. Then, *let that purpose fuel your passion.*

 *"Purpose fuels Passion."*

I particularly liked this phrase, because the use of the word "fuels" ties back into last week's discussion of recharging. We need to remember that *our software solutions help thousands of nonprofits raise **hundreds of millions** of dollars for their causes.* We're really excited about the launch of the Virtual Fundraising Solution, but we can't forget that we are already powering hundreds of virtual fundraising events each and every week with our current auction and event software, peer-to-peer, and Text2Give solutions. It's mind-blowing to see the breadth and diversity of the causes we serve.

Justice and rights, disabilities, health and hospitals, cancer, Crohn's, education, arts, and so much more. Just this past week, we helped to power 269 events that raised more than $12 million in proceeds!

Let the **purpose of what we do drive your passion.**

"We are passionate."

FEARLESS FUNDRAISING IN ACTION

Ronald McDonald House of Kansas City—Red Shoe Shindig

Last week, Ronald McDonald House of Kansas City challenged their community to make 2020 a banner year for their Red Shoe Shindig. The week-long festivities kicked off with virtual trivia, social media photo challenges, and registration/pre-bidding contests to drive activity leading up to their livestreamed event. They brought their annual Red Shoe Shindig Gala to the online world broadcasting over our Virtual Fundraising Solution with dueling piano entertainment, silent auction, raffle, and live appeal. The reimagined event crushed its fundraising goal to help the local Ronald McDonald House continue to keep serving families as their services have adapted to the COVID pandemic.

In closing, I would like to share another quote. This one comes from Kara Goldin, the founder of Hint fruit-infused water company. In a remarkable "3 for 4" on our values (I'm enjoying watching the baseball playoffs!), Kara says, "I would take Passion, Curiosity, and Commitment over experience any day of the week." We agree Kara! Good news for us, we don't have to sacrifice experience!! Haha!!

Let your purpose drive your passion.

Next week—"We are curious."

We are passionate!

Steve

October 15, 2020

we are curious.

Last week we did a deep dive on our first value—"We are passionate." This week's discussion around our second value "We are curious" must begin with that.

It is our *passion* (fueled by our purpose) that drives us to be *curious*.

Without passion, we may lose interest. We may not be driven to seek answers.

To be curious is to be eager to learn, to explore, to discover. To seek knowledge and solutions.

The "action statement" that accompanies our second value "We are curious" is:

Always be open, explore, and learn. It's our curiosity that drives us to think creatively and deliver innovative solutions. We learn from each other and our customers as we grow our expertise and solve for the future needs of donors and nonprofits.

As the pandemic has so clearly taught us, we must continue to be curious and seek new solutions. We have to learn from our customers (listen to them) and from each other to continue to *innovate* and deliver solutions for their changing needs.

Funny thing though, I'd be willing to wager that a lot of us have had a "mixed" relationship with curiosity as we've grown to adulthood—particularly the baby boomers and the Gen X'ers among us. As I'll note later, the millennials (Gen Y) and definitely Gen Z do not in general have this issue.

Remember, "Curiosity killed the cat." Whoa! Beware the dangers of asking too many questions!

Remember Curious George? He was the lovable, curious monkey who couldn't help his curiosity. What happened to him? In various stories (that all ended happily thank goodness) he floods a house, gets carried off by a kite, breaks a leg, crashes on a bike, and passes out after inhaling ether!!

A lot can go wrong if you're curious apparently. "It's dangerous." NO. Break that pattern!!

For those parents out there, how many times can your children ask you, "Why?" A lot, right?! For many, that curiosity fades over time.

So, let's be more like our kids! ☺ Keep asking, "Why" until we find the root cause. This will drive us to continue to find innovative solutions to our customers' issues. It will also drive us to find new ways to run, grow, and scale our own business.

Ask, "Why?" Experiment. Take some risks. Ask more questions.

Create a safe environment for it. Eliminate the fear. Cultivate challenges.

Now to that millennials point I made earlier. I had the opportunity to interview at least six candidates for the Orr Fellowship program last year. Orr Fellows are generally just completing an undergraduate program (late Gen Y or early Z). The OneCause Values were fresh, and so Dan and I were asking them which value resonated most with them.

Far and away, "**We are curious**" resonated more than the others. To the credit of the aforementioned boomers and Gen X'ers, although we might have been raised to be more cautious, our kids are curious!

This bodes well for our future.

It also turns out that curious people generally develop better relationships with others.

Dale Carnegie has been attributed to the saying: *"To be interesting, be interested."*

I like this, but it seems a bit self-serving/selfish—perhaps even insincere.

A different twist to the concept comes from the original advice columnist herself Ann Landers: *"Being interested is more important than being interesting."*

Be interested. Be curious.

We'll develop a deeper connection with our customers by being curious about their unmet needs, their pain points.

We'll be better product managers, software developers, salespeople, and customer advocates the more we demonstrate curiosity and seek knowledge.

And from THE most interesting man in the world . . . "Stay Curious, My Friends."

"We are curious."

FEARLESS FUNDRAISING IN ACTION
2020 Children's Right Challenge—#1NATION4Children
This weekend, Children's Rights launched their #1NATION4CHILDREN campaign with a two-week national fitness challenge hosted on Strava. An integral part of the campaign is to bring awareness to the needs of kids languishing in child welfare systems. Their goal is to collectively log 500,000 hours of fitness (cycling, running, walking, swimming, yoga, etc.) and raise funds through Individual Challenge Ambassadors and Corporate Sponsors & Teams to represent the half a million kids in foster care in the United States. Challenge participants will be celebrated in a Virtual Benefit on November 18th featuring Cyndi Lauper. Five days into the campaign and they already have 92,000' participants in their Strava challenge with 176 Challenge Ambassadors actively raising money for Children's Rights. Stay tuned to this one as they drive towards their goal.

QUOTE OF THE WEEK

"You are wonderful more than I can say, and you helped me on what has been a very difficult process but made it a breeze to move companies and be there for my every beck and call."

—Dara, Development Director, AZCEND

The deeper we dive into our values, the more pertinent and meaningful they become.

We are passionate.

We are curious.

Next week—"We are helpful."

Stay curious my friends,

Steve

LEADERSHIP LESSONS

- **Values build cultures**
  Reaffirming core values is an important way to unite an organization. It reminds everyone of their shared purpose, common goals, and collective mindsets. It's the fabric that ties, binds, and buoys in times of change.

- **Values shape outcomes**
  Values are more than vague statements of intent. They are practical guides that can serve as benchmarks for assessing ideas, actions, and performance. Use them as a regular point of reference to help align individual behavior and organizational strategy.

- **Live out your values**

  As a leader, "living your values" isn't just a well-meaning catchphrase. It's a structural tool for shaping a living and changing organization. If you don't model your values in your own behavior and attitudes, don't expect anyone else to take them seriously.

CHAPTER 8

Who We Are (Part II)
Helpful and Committed

When we crafted the OneCause Values, everyone working on the project was determined they should be more than just slogans. It's easy to be cynical about these things. We've all seen mission and values statements that look like they were crafted by a piece of jargon creation software.

Start with "Saving the World," add a few unsubstantiated claims and immeasurable goals, and let the algorithms do their work. A few moments later, out pops a stale statement of corporate vision.

But when a set of values genuinely reflects the core identity and aspirations of a business and its mission, they become more than just empty words. They are a beacon that lights the way forward and offers comfort and inspiration in tough times.

One of my goals in writing about our values was to reinforce the culture that makes OneCause unique. When we first developed these values, I joked that we needed something meaningful, not just catchy phrases to slap on coffee mugs and stationery.

Now as we finished six months of the biggest work-from-home experiment the world had ever seen, I was thinking, "Wow! We don't even have the coffee mugs and posters around the office to remind us anymore!"

My updates were one of the few regular touchpoints connecting every member of the OneCause Nation. It seemed important to use the updates to support our culture and ways of thinking and keep everyone rallied around our shared purpose.

The motivation didn't come from a sense that we were falling apart or that we weren't living up to our expectations. In fact, I was amazed by how seamless the transition to remote working had been and by how much we continued to accomplish without a physical hub to tie everyone together. My purpose was to reinforce our values as a tool for handling the situation we were facing now, as shared frameworks for thinking that we could all actively apply to steer our planning, decisions, and actions.

Our values give us objective criteria that help us evaluate whether we're working in the right way toward the right goals. If I come up with an idea, someone might call me on a value: "Hey Steve, if we take that action, is it really consistent with being curious?" That's not a personal criticism. It's a useful question to check whether what we are doing really aligns with what we *should* be doing. Our values define our culture by shaping and directing our attitudes *and* our actions.

This is one of the reasons I've always loved having, *"We are helpful"* as a value. It says so much about who we strive to be as individuals and about our goals as a team. And the way it emerged was completely organic. In the process of defining our values, we surveyed everyone on the OneCause team asking some essential questions:

- "What does it mean to be OneCause?"
- "What do we bring to our customers that makes us who we are?"

When we pulled together the answers, the word "helpful" stood out loud and clear.

As a company, we help others achieve their goals. We don't reach out to donors. We don't raise money. We don't produce the events. Our role is to *help* nonprofits empower their mission through our software, our people, and our resources. That's what OneCause is all about, and every single member of the OneCause Nation knows it.

In itself, helpfulness is clearly essential. But what's also amazing about putting the spotlight on the value of helpfulness is that it ends up turning inward as well. It's hard to express what a pleasure it is to work with people who want to be helpful to each other, who go into meetings asking, "How can I help get that done?" OneCause employees treat each other with the same consideration we give the nonprofits we work with.

Important as each individual value is, it's when they come together that they really come alive. The list isn't arranged at random. There's a chronology to it, with each one preparing the way for and feeding into the next.

- We are passionate.
- We are curious.
- We are helpful.
- We are committed.

Our purpose and passion drive us to be curious.

Our curiosity seeks out solutions for our customers so we can be helpful to them.

And our desire to help leads us to be committed to seeing the work through to the very end, whatever that end might be.

Our commitment—to the nonprofits we work for and to each other—ties everything together. It's that special something in our culture that turns ideas into results and plans into actions. It strengthens the bonds we have to each other even when things are hard. And it's our values that proved to be the most critical for seeing us through the pandemic.

October 23, 2020
we are helpful.

I love our values. They're like good food. They are good by themselves, but sometimes even better in combination with each other.

Also, they make more sense and create more joy in the proper
order and sequence.

They should also be in the proper context for full pleasure and
enjoyment.

As I noted a couple of weeks ago in discussing our first value,
"We are passionate"—Passion is fueled by our Purpose. The context
of our values flows from our Purpose as articulated in our Vision
and our Mission.

It's in the context of our Vision of *"Building Better Tomorrows"*
and our Mission of *". . . helping nonprofits to connect with more
supporters and raise more money . . ."* where our values really begin.

Fueled by our purpose,

"We are passionate."

That passion drives us to seek knowledge, learn, and ask why.

"We are curious."

With a curious mind, we engage with our customers, ask questions, understand their needs, and create innovative solutions to
their needs.

"We are helpful."

The action statement accompanying our third value of "We are
helpful" is this:

*Jump in, work together, and make it better. We go above
and beyond to help our nonprofit customers succeed and further their causes. We live our helpfulness every day, by working*

across departments, sharing knowledge, and coming together to deliver seamless experiences.

You may not remember, but the "word cloud" exercise that the entire company participated in to connect with our values-setting process reflected "Helpful" as the leading word to describe what it meant to be a OneCauser.

I want to point out that our action statement is not only about helping our customers succeed, it's about working together, sharing knowledge, and coming together as a team to deliver that customer experience.

This is more difficult in a WFH environment. We have to work harder. We have to be more purposeful and deliberate in our collaboration, teamwork, and communications.

There's a really important string I want to pull here—this might be a bit controversial.

Get ready. Please give me your thoughts.

The helpfulness that I'm talking about is not altruism. Altruism is behavior that benefits another at a cost to oneself. Our helpfulness is provided to *add value* and *create value*.

Our collective team has years of fundraising experience, and our innovative products reflect the learnings and experience of more than 40,000 fundraising campaigns for 10,000 different nonprofits spanning over a decade.

We're ready to help our customers realize their full potential as Fearless Fundraisers. We put our customers and their causes first.

By lifting them up and helping them be successful, we help ourselves grow, prosper and secure our future. We want to be around for a very long time and also continue to deliver the service and innovative products they have come to rely on through the years.

Back when I was selling "Consultative Services" for Coopers & Lybrand, I used to listen to Zig Ziglar cassette tapes in my smoking hot '83 Toyota Celica. Ah, the good old days . . .

Thinking on this, I was reminded of a Zig Ziglar quote:

> *"If you help people get what they want,*
> *they will help you get what you want."*

If we helped others without value in return, we would not be in business very long.

Let's also look at the notion of Servant Leadership. This is the concept of serving others first before yourself. This is the kind of helpfulness we should aspire to master. The Servant Leader puts the needs of others first (serves).

I serve as CEO of OneCause.

OneCause serves the needs of our customers.

Together, we grow, prosper, flourish, and create shared value.

I found this quote by Kurt Uhlir:

> *"Ultimately, I just want to help people and believe we*
> *have to work crazy hard to make the future happen."*

Any one of us could have said that. That's what we do every day. Help people. Work crazy hard. Shape our future.

If you've not spent much time in understanding the notion of Servant Leadership, here is a viewpoint provided by Uhlir:

10 Qualities of a Servant Leader

L **Listening**
A deep commitment to listening intently to others. Ask clarifying questions and reflect what they hear from others.

E **Empathizing**
Seek to understand people's feelings about the situation. Assume good intentions. Does not limit holding people accountable.

A **Acting intentionally**
A well-developed self-awareness combined with general awareness enables you to make intentional, wise actions.

D **Dedicating time for others**
Actively look for ways to build relationships with others and foster a sense of community.

E **Empowering others**
Hire capable people and show them the way. Recognize that we have surrounded ourselves with them for a reason.

R **Removing obstacles**
Identify the resources others need to succeed. Look for organizational and situational barriers you can remove to help the team.

S **Serving others**
Approach people as a steward trusted to help them become their best and grow to better enable the team to reach its goals.

H **Helping with humility**
Seeks to convince others rather than coerce compliance. Effectively build consensus within groups and individuals.

I **Interact with integrity**
Radiates openness and authenticity. Knows that how the outcome is achieved matters as much or more than the outcome.

P **Persevering**
Keep a steady course in spite of difficulties, obstacles, or discouragement. Actively looks for ways to encourage others.

MAM
Made in America Movement

Chief Servants
Kurt Uhlir

Reprinted with permission.

Just like everything I present each week, I want to get you to think. I've never described myself as a Servant Leader, or subscribed to that particular doctrine, but there is a lot that resonates here.

Finally, I don't want you to think that I don't believe in selfless acts. I do. I believe that they can make you feel better. And in that sense, they do create value.

"We are passionate."

"We are curious."

"We are helpful."

Next week . . . "We are committed."

FEARLESS FUNDRAISING IN ACTION
United Way for Southeastern Michigan—Virtual Marathon

The United Way for Southeastern Michigan launched their Run United Virtual Marathon to support efforts to close the digital divide for Detroit students, providing them with laptops, internet access, and other technology supports.

From Sept. 16 through Oct. 17, United Way encouraged participants to log at least 25 miles on their own through the integrated Strava app, completing the final 1.2 miles together with a virtual "race" on Oct. 18. Participants earned points for posting photos and videos, signing up to volunteer, tracking their miles in the Strava app, recruiting their friends, and reaching fundraising milestones. The group of 647 participants far exceeded their goal of 10,000 miles, clocking in a whopping 22,565 miles.

The Run United 2020 surpassed its fundraising goal by 119%, raising money to equip 893 Detroit students with the technology they need to learn.

QUOTE OF THE WEEK

"OneCause has helped us overcome the challenge of changing our event from a face-to-face luncheon to a virtual one. We have exceeded the sponsorship goal and are on our way to exceeding the overall goal! I highly recommend OneCause! This will be our 12th Holiday Luncheon with Friends and the pandemic created an opportunity for us to re-think the presentation. With OneCause's help, we are preparing the website for our silent auction and program on the day of the event. Other than the normal hiccups of learning a new program, we have swiftly moved from a face-to-face special event to an online venue. We anticipate that we will see a huge increase in participation—normal attendance is around 210-240 but all indicators point to a range of 600-800 this year. With increased participation, comes increased fundraising. In these unprecedented days, it is critical that we meet the event's goal, and exceeding it will be even better!"

—Another Happy G2 Crowd Reviewer

Until next week.

Stay helpful my friends,

Steve

October 31, 2020

we are committed.

*"Feeling dedication and loyalty to a cause, activity, or job;
wholeheartedly dedicated."*

—Oxford English Dictionary

*"Bound or obligated to a person or thing,
as by pledge or assurance; devoted."*

—dictionary.com

*"Loyal to a belief, organization, or group,
and willing to work hard for it."*

—Macmillan Dictionary

I hope that you've enjoyed our last few weeks of deep diving into our company values. I have to say, I've learned something along the way!

"We are passionate."

"We are curious."

"We are helpful."

. . . and finally

"We are committed."

We conceptualized our values in a different place and time. Yet, they seem so appropriate for today.

Again,

Fueled by our Purpose,

"We are passionate."

That passion drives us to seek knowledge, learn, and ask why.

"We are curious."

With a curious mind, we engage with our customers, ask questions, understand their needs, and create innovative solutions to their needs.

"We are helpful."

Our dedication, our loyalty, and our beliefs in *our cause* and *the causes that we serve* compel us to work hard and see challenges through to the end.

"We are committed."

Our action statement accompanying our value of "We are committed" says this:

> We see it through to the finish. We're committed to our nonprofit partners' success from the first touch-point and even beyond when the final giving results are tallied. We're committed to our shared success and to delivering on the OneCause mission.

The statement above supports the statement that I made last week. We are indeed committed to our customers' success, but we're equally committed to *shared success* and achieving our own Mission.

If all of this sounds kinda like parenting, it is. Parrish and I had a great conversation about this last week after my update about "We are helpful."

Parents are driven by purpose: a better life for their children. That purpose drives their passion, their curiosity to seek more, and their helpfulness to guide, develop, and show the way.

But it can't be ALL about their children. They also have the responsibility of being a good spouse, friend, partner, and/or businessperson. We also have the responsibility to simply be a good person. To make a positive impact on the world while we're here.

The job of a parent is never done.

Our job serving our customers and their causes is never done.

Our action statement says, "*We see it through to the finish.*" But, if we're really succeeding, there is no finish. That in itself is exhilarating and potentially exhausting at the same time.

Because of this, we have to take moments and celebrate successes along the way. Again, the parenting analogy is appropriate:

- Sleeping through the night for the first time.
- Toilet training.
- Walking, riding a bike, driving a car.
- Education and sports achievements.
- Going off to college.
- Leaving the nest.

Each one of these milestones creates a moment to celebrate, to pause and reflect. A moment to take a breath and prepare for the next phase.

We need to do the same.

Let's take a moment and be grateful.

We must stay committed to seeing it through.

In closing and on a personal note, "We are committed" is the value that resonates most with me.

As I reflect on my career, I can say that I have seen my greatest success in being the person still standing to carry the ball over the goal line. It's not very glamorous. But it feels good.

This year has thrown a lot at us. I am committed to you. I am committed to OneCause.

So, I generally include a quote from some notable figure in my weekly updates. This week, the quote comes from that "one hit wonder" from Minneapolis—*Semisonic* in their 1998 hit "Closing Time."

"Every new beginning comes from some other beginning's end."

Just like parenting, we are never really "finished." But, we can continue to deliver successive successes, taking a moment to celebrate our victories and moving on to our next challenge.

"We are committed."
To our customers, our families, our loved ones, ourselves, and our OneCause family.

FEARLESS FUNDRAISING IN ACTION
Make-A-Wish Maine—Wish Night 2020
With more than 100 wish children waiting for their wishes (30 of which were postponed due to COVID), Make-A-Wish Maine hosted their first Virtual Wish Night to raise the critical funds needed to be able to grant wishes at an unprecedented rate when it's safe again for wish kids to realize their wishes in the public domain.

Supporters created their own at-home Wish Night with party-in-place packages and a pre-event virtual Happy Hour as they tuned in via Facebook Live and YouTube Live for the virtual event. The 30-minute livestreamed program celebrated the 1,600th wish granted by Make-A-Wish Maine and featured details on auction packages, a behind-the-scenes look at how a wish comes true, and the Fund-A-Wish appeal.

The 2020 virtual event was their highest grossing Wish Night yet, reaching more than 1,500 views on Facebook and climbing to incredible proceeds.

QUOTE OF THE WEEK

"OneCause jumped right on the virtual event platform creation right when the pandemic began to set in. As this impacted thousands of nonprofits around the country, OneCause set up a platform that has given us the ability to run successful events in a virtual space—something I'm not sure we could have pulled off without their partnership."

—G2 Crowd Review

Happy Halloween to everyone! Just like everything these days, it's a different feeling than ever before.

It's another milestone in our journey together.

"We are passionate."

"We are curious."

"We are helpful."

And finally . . .

"We are committed."

Congratulations on a successful third quarter!

Let's see 2020 through to the end—finish strong and build momentum for 2021!

Stay committed!

Steve

LEADERSHIP LESSONS

- **Find purpose in serving others**
  Purpose is what gives us passion and drives us forward. Service to others is a renewable resource for motivation and is particularly important in times of crisis. By building networks of service through which we help our colleagues and our customers, we have a way to create shared value and flourish together.

- **Helpfulness doesn't have to come at a cost**
  People often treat being helpful as a zero-sum game: "If I help you, that comes at a cost to me." But that's a narrow view. The best type of helpfulness creates or adds value. By finding ways to do things better and more effectively, we help our fearless fundraisers *and* ourselves.

- **The finish isn't the end**
  Being committed doesn't just mean seeing projects through to their conclusion. It means carrying the wisdom you have acquired forward and applying it in pursuit of your next goal. Pause, celebrate what you have achieved, and then move forward to the next challenge because commitment, by its very nature, doesn't end.

CHAPTER 9

Moral Leadership in Divided Times

On September 18, 2020, we lost a great American. Ruth Bader Ginsburg was a titan of the legal landscape in this country—a pioneering women's rights activist and an Associate Justice of the Supreme Court for more than quarter of a century.

The day after I heard the news, I sent out a short note to everyone at OneCause acknowledging her passing. That's not something I do often. In fact, the only other times have been when musical heroes of mine have "left the stage" forever. But no matter what your politics, RBG was an icon, a leader who fought for what she believed in, even when it was hard, challenging, or contentious. She spoke of leadership as "leaving tracks" and leaving "the world a little better for your being there." At OneCause, we believe in these ideals about legacy and impact. It felt right to recognize her achievements.

There was another reason RBG's passing impacted me personally: she represented a time when public life was much less divided than it is today, a time when disagreements were more collegial, more decorous, more civilized. Ginsburg was nominated by a Democratic president at the suggestion of a Republican senator. Her confirmation hearings were largely polite and restrained. She was confirmed with a huge bipartisan majority, with just three senators voting against. It was almost another world.

Now Supreme Court justices are typically treated as political figures, aligned, if not directly affiliated, with the party that nominated them. In fact, we've become so polarized that I hesitated to send my email. I knew that there were some, perhaps even many, who wouldn't mourn the passing of a "liberal" judge. Would it be divisive, I wondered, to honor someone associated with one side of the political divide?

I clicked Send. Our country is more divided now than it has been at any other time in my life. But I wasn't willing to be paralyzed by that division. There are other ways forward.

The importance of finding those other paths was brought home again and again in the months that followed RBG's death. The presidential election, its contested aftermath, and the events of January 6th made it clear that our society is deeply fractured when it comes to politics. Some commentators have even suggested that we have passed the point of no return. I don't believe that for a minute. Nonprofits and their teams show us many models of cooperation that cut across party lines. We see these models in campaigns, fundraisers, and events that reach toward a common good, a shared mission, or a united goal. And I see this same spirit every day at OneCause.

Pessimism about where we are now and what comes after is a road that only leads into the darkness. Hopeful optimism is the path that takes us back to the light. And as I wrote my updates in the months before and after the election, I felt that I had a duty both to choose hope and to communicate my reasons for that choice.

My goal in writing was to reassure my fellow OneCausers, to let them know that I shared their worries but believed in a better tomorrow. But taking a little time to reflect on what we had built together and how to sustain it was a source of inspiration for me as well. It reminded me that when people share a meaningful vision, a goal, a cause, what they have in common is far more powerful than the points of difference that might separate them. There is something both simple and profound in that realization.

At OneCause, the commitment to a shared vision is built into everything we do. As a team dedicated to serving *all* causes, we have a responsibility—individually and collectively—to reject the idea that our society is so fractured that we can't support people on all sides. We unite around a common vision and mission with the goal of creating better tomorrows. It's the only way we can do our jobs. What we share *has* to come first. It *has* to take priority over what separates us.

The model of working in pursuit of a common vision isn't unique to OneCause. It's what this country was built on, and it plays out minute by minute and hour by hour in communities and workplaces coast to coast. The fact that we can work together in this way is a source of hope. But we have to choose to be hopeful. We have to choose to share a common experience.

An important goal in my updates was to encourage people to make this choice. We are all responsible for leading ourselves every day, for making choices and choosing how we respond to the uncertainty in the world. Getting past partisan ideologies starts with a choice. It starts with the decision to value something shared, something common as we value what unites us more than what divides us.

As I thought about the political turmoil and the COVID pandemic, I began to see the decision facing us all as a battle to be fought. But this wasn't a battle against others. It was a battle for an ideal.

We had to choose to fight the virus together.

We had to choose to fight against the divisions in our society.

We had to choose to fight for unity and a shared view of a better world.

For me, OneCause was the symbol of that choice. OneCause is my "why." It's the banner I march under, shoulder to shoulder with the rest of the OneCause Nation. Our shared worldview offers us all a filter for understanding events and responding to them in a positive way. *That* is our rallying cry. We are all united by this one mission; we are brought together by this one shared cause.

September 19, 2020

RIP RBG

We lost an icon. A true champion of justice.

Love this quote. Really connects with my message yesterday regarding what it means to be a thought leader.

Steve

"Fight for the things you care about, but do it in a way that will lead others to join you."

Ruth Bader Ginsburg

November 6, 2020

what's next?

I really enjoyed diving deeper into our values for the past four weeks. I hope you enjoyed it too.

I found myself thinking, "Ok Steve, what's next?"

I had four weeks of solid content. Established themes. Inspiration. Uh oh! Did I get lazy?

"What's next, Steve?"

This week has been something of an emotional roller coaster. I stayed up way too late on Tuesday to see the election results come in. They did for a while and then they just froze. I went to bed at 235 to 213, and I woke up to 235 to 213.

We're starting to see some progress (it's now Thursday night).

What's next?

Recounts, lawsuits, accusations, social media tweets, posturing, and more division.

It will end. But . . .

What's next?

We're still very broken.

- Healthcare
- Climate change
- Economic uncertainty
- Joblessness
- Racial and social injustice
- Discrimination
- Homelessness
- Poverty
- Food insecurity

Oh, yeah. We're still in the middle of a Global Pandemic that is 8 months old and arguably worsening.

What's next?

Which of these sound better to you?

Hope. Healing. Honor. Humanity. Humility.

Or

Hate. Hubris. Hostility.

You guys know I love my alliteration!!

Last week I talked about being **committed**. Committed to see things through. I also acknowledged that sometimes it feels like our job is never done. So, we have to find milestones along the way to mark our journey. Take a breath and get ready for what's next.

I'm reminded of Jeff Bezos' "Day 1 Mindset." Bezos has become less popular these days. We love to build our heroes up just to tear them down sometimes. Whatever you think of him, he's been wildly successful—most likely beyond even *his* wildest dreams. His Day 1 Mindset is:

> *"Treat every day like it's the first day of your start-up.*
> *Keep your entrepreneurial mindset."*

The building his office is in is called Day 1, and there is a plaque that reads:

> *"There's so much stuff that has yet to be invented.*
> *There's so much new that's going to happen."*

Whatever you think of Bezos, think Day 1. Tomorrow is Day 1 of "What's next?" What's next for OneCause and for our country? We will continue to innovate, delight our customers, take calculated risks, aspire to greatness, and likely make some mistakes along the way.

I choose **hope**.

This is why I have hope for 2021, and why every day will be Day 1 toward the return of a growing and prosperous OneCause:

1. After much division, there will be resolution of our presidential leadership choice. We are clearly still divided as a country. The role of that person will be to bring us back together to work on the long list of issues we have to face as a country with healing grace.

2. There will be a resolution of our Congressional elections, and they will pass a Fiscal Stimulus package to bring much-needed support for our economy.

3. There will be positive progress on a COVID vaccine which will give us all greater confidence for a return to [new] normalcy in the second half of 2021.

> *"I think if you do something, and it turns out pretty good, then you should go do something else wonderful, not dwell on it for too long. Just figure out what's next."*
> Steve Jobs

We've done some things that have turned out pretty good. We've been remarkably resilient in 2020. Let's not dwell on that. Let's go do something truly innovative and wonderful in 2021!

So, take a breath and get ready for Day 1 of *"What's next?"*

With,

Healing. Humility. Hope.

FEARLESS FUNDRAISING IN ACTION
Sunrise Association—SunriseLIVE!
Recognizing there was no safe way to gather in-person, Sunrise Association decided to virtualize their 2020 fundraising events. For the first time, three philanthropic communities were brought

together for one special event as they combined the annual Dare to Dream with two other events, Friends of Sunrise and Rock the River, as a part of the reimagined SunriseLIVE! virtual event.

Celebrity emcee Andy Cohen led supporters through an inspiring evening including a pre-show honoring Sunrise Alumni working on front lines of the COVID crisis, musical performances, camper stories, and an exciting silent auction and live appeal. Supporters were encouraged to host their own watch parties and text to register to join in the bidding and donation appeal.

Sunrise Association was blown away as the number of live viewers was way above their expectations and they more than doubled their fundraising goal, to bring joy to children with cancer and their siblings through their magical day camps, year-round activities, and in-hospital programs, all free of charge.

QUOTE OF THE WEEK

"It was SO easy to input silent auction items. I love that we could stream the event directly on to the OneCause platform. The texting ability is SO helpful!"

—Rachel, Education and Outreach Coordinator, New Life Adoptions

Many of us will be OK seeing this week in the rearview mirror. It's been very emotional. We are not done, but just like the stock market—certainty is better than uncertainty.

Let's get ready for Day 1—the first day toward the answer to "What's next?" for OneCause and for our Country!!

Onward!

Steve

November 14, 2020

Happy Saturday OneCause Nation!

Before we begin . . .
I'd like to welcome *The Economist* to our world of hope. ☺ Just last week, I wrote the words "I choose hope." And now this week, on the cover page of *The Economist*—spotlighting the very good news released on Monday by Pfizer regarding its COVID vaccine—were the words: "*Suddenly hope.*"

Despite what appears to be a new surge in COVID cases around the country, there is "hope" for the long term in our fight against the pandemic.

But make no mistake, it is a **fight.**

covid. combat. connection.

COVID.
COVID-19 ("COVID") invaded and attacked our country. There's no other way of saying it. COVID has wrought the greatest destruction to the US, and likely the world, of any single event in modern history.

Deaths, disease, healthcare costs, job loss, destruction of companies and entire industries, the emerging mental health crisis, and more. It has not finished with us.

We are being told that "Winter is coming" and yes, it might already be here.

A "tough winter."
—Fauci
A "dark winter."
—Biden

If I had to give COVID a face, it would be the Night King from Game of Thrones.

We have to continue to be vigilant. This is not over. Books aren't being written. Stories cannot be told. Movie rights have not been sold. We're not done.

We are still "in this." The story does not have an ending. Yet.

combat.

We are at war with COVID. Just in case you haven't seen these statistics, they are sobering . . .

WAR	U.S. DEATHS
World War II	405,399
World War I	116,516
Vietnam	58,220
Korea	36,574
Iraq, Afghanistan	7,053

COVID-19
242,000 and we're not done.
(based on November 2020 data)

We can argue facts and figures all day about the number of cases, hospitalizations, ICUs, ventilators, testing, contact tracing, etc. We can even argue about the "true" cause of death by quoting "co-morbidities" like cancer, kidney disease, obesity, heart conditions, type 2 diabetes, etc. In fact, we may never get at the "truth."

US deaths attributed to COVID-19 are greater than all wars since WWII.

The truth is that people are dying, our economy has been devastated, our own business at OneCause has been hit hard, and some industries like the live concert/music business may take years to recover—if they ever can.

We are in active combat.

Be vigilant. Wear your mask. This might seem like a helplessly little thing to do, but believe me, it can make a difference. We cannot stop COVID (without a vaccine), but we can do everything in our power to slow its spread.

WWII helmets weren't intended to stop bullets, but I bet the people who were wearing one were glad they did!!

This week has been mixed. The amazing news about the Pfizer vaccine was followed by good news from Indy's own Eli Lilly with their antiviral treatment bamlanivimab receiving emergency use authorization.

But what followed was more bad news about rising case levels and resulting draconian actions taken by the City of Chicago to "lock down" its citizens (including my daughter) by "advisory."

Imagery from the Churchill War Rooms in downtown London come to mind. (If you are in London someday again and passionate about history, I highly recommend it.)

Hunker down. Bunker in. Stay inside. Essential travel only. Night-time curfews. Wartime.

connection.
Herein is the silver lining. We are in this together. When a group of people have a significant shared experience, they form a bond that sometimes lasts for a lifetime.

I feel a greater connection to you for sharing this experience with me.

If you have a cool teal OneCause t-shirt, you were with us in the Summer of 2020. "The Summer of COVID."

We will have experienced this together. We are connected—in some sense forever.

Teammates on a championship team. A mission trip. A spiritual experience.

Survivors of a disaster. Liberated prisoners of war. Soldiers surviving combat.

We will all have our COVID survival stories to tell.

We are connected.

What happens next, right? I'll continue to do my part to help lead our company through the coming "winter." I will stay open, transparent, and continue to communicate with you.

I want to ask you for the same. Remember your OneCause family. We are in the midst of a shared experience, but we all deal with it differently. Someone out there might need a Slack message, a text, or a call. If you haven't talked to someone in a while, reach out and do so. It might be just what they needed.

It's Friday night, and I'm alone at the office cranking *Cowboy Song* by Thin Lizzy off of their *Jailbreak* album. Yes! Kelly just told me that we got our #1 choice for the Orr Fellowship!! Yes!! Why wouldn't we?

We are OneCause Nation.

FEARLESS FUNDRAISING IN ACTION

TeamMates Mentoring Program—Tailgate Gala

The annual TeamMates Gala funds about 1/3 of the organization's Mentoring Program that supports 170 school districts across 5 states. Planning a mission critical event like this during a pandemic was challenging, but the TeamMates Gala committee was committed to creating an inspiring and enjoyable virtual TeamMates Tailgate Gala with actor and comedian Bill Murray, investor Warren Buffett, and TeamMates founder Coach Tom Osborne.

Using our Virtual Fundraising Solution, they exceeded their fundraising goal prior to the start of the livestreamed gala, from ticket sales, sponsorship, and donations. The gala livestream featured a silent auction with Warren Buffet-autographed dollar bills going for impressive sums and a live auction with unique Bill Murray and Tom Osborne inspired items including a Caddy Shack themed golf cart. The event culminated with a live appeal and donation match. The livestream event was a huge success surpassing its goal to help inspire youth to reach their full potential through mentoring.

Well, it's now Saturday morning, and I'm watching the 3rd round of "The Masters." It's November 14th! Not the second Sunday of April. What the blank??!!

Just another example of the topsy turvy world that is 2020. As we get closer to the end of the year, I have to say I am looking forward to saying goodbye to 2020.

Not that anything magical is going to happen on January 1, 2021, but I do have **hope** for a better tomorrow.

With hope,

Steve

January 7, 2021

A Note from Steve

OneCause Nation:

In challenging times, **unity, above all**, is of the most importance.

We as a company and as a country must come together in the wake of the disturbing events at our nation's Capitol yesterday. As I have said many times before, while we cannot always control the events and circumstances around us, we can control how we react to them.

At OneCause we rally around our shared purpose. We stand for building better tomorrows. As a team, we remain committed to our core values that guide and inspire us.

Many of you may be experiencing feelings of angst and unrest today. **Please know we're here for you.** If you're struggling or need to talk to someone, reach out to HR, your manager, or a colleague. Our team is strong, and we are always here to support one another.

Together we will move forward. Our elected leaders in government showed us yesterday the importance of continuing on. We live in a great democracy, and we must let that democracy work.

At OneCause we have a shared purpose to drive positive impact and create social good.

What we do now matters. **Our team is resilient—you continue to show me that every day.**

Forever grateful for our amazing team.

Onward,

Steve

LEADERSHIP LESSONS

- **Choose togetherness**

  In an increasingly partisan world, communicating across lines of conflict is an essential part of leadership. Your role is to encourage your team to choose a common purpose that finds ways to unite, while creating a safe space for honest and authentic dialogue.

- **Choose inclusivity**

  When tackling difficult issues, empathy and an open heart are essential for understanding what matters to people and why. Communication needs to be inclusive rather than confrontational, even when you are taking a stand on an issue. Seek to build bridges, foster dialogue, and, most of all, listen to every viewpoint.

- **Choose what's right**

  Unity and agreement are important goals. But when leaders and organizations are committed to living their values, they won't see eye to eye with everyone. Sometimes, you will have to speak up even if you know that doing so will make some people uncomfortable. At these times, rely on your mission and your core values to guide your decisions, actions, and leadership.

CHAPTER 10

The Future of Work

When the OneCause team began to work from home in March 2020, it was an emergency measure, a necessity forced on us by the threat of the pandemic. At the time, I think we all assumed that this new situation was a temporary change that would disrupt our normal way of working for a few weeks or a few months at most. Then, once COVID was under control, everything would return to normal.

When we first sent everyone home, the executive management team anticipated a drop in productivity. It wasn't that we didn't trust our team members. On the contrary, with nearly a third of OneCause Nation already in distributed roles outside the office environment, we knew our people didn't need direct supervision to work effectively. The truth is, after spending most of our working lives in traditional offices, we had simply internalized certain assumptions about the optimal way to do business. As it turned out, we were wrong in important respects.

As 2020 progressed, it became increasingly clear that we wouldn't be returning to our old way of working any time soon. Instead, we would have to adapt to a new normal that would be with us for many months more, and potentially for years. Our initial disaster management response was to see the challenge as a "problem" to be "solved." Six months later, we had a very different perspective on both what was possible and what was desirable.

By September 2020, we knew that OneCause could operate successfully without an "office first" mentality. The team had shown that we could engineer new products, pivot the company, grow our customer base, and generally thrive rather than just survive in this new environment. More than that, our internal surveys were telling us that most OneCausers liked at least some features of their new working lives. We weren't just making the best of a bad situation. We were seeing working practices evolve in positive new directions.

Going "back to the office" no longer seemed the natural goal it had once been. So, we decided to go forward instead. By shaking up our assumptions, the pandemic had delivered us a COVID silver lining. We were given a once-in-a-lifetime opportunity to re-examine the way we worked from the ground up. And I was determined that we would grasp it with both hands.

Our review of working practices was the most far-reaching I have ever been engaged in. In the process, we carried out a vision casting of what the future of work would look like at every level of our organization. We decided to look at every possibility. No assumption was sacred. The human needs of our team would be front and center in our planning. At the same time, we knew that we needed to be careful and deliberate. You don't overturn long-held beliefs and working norms on a whim, and it was vital that we got this right.

We had been discussing the subject internally for three or four months before I addressed it in an update. The timing was far from perfect. In February 2021, we hadn't yet finished pinning down all the details of the review. We had a good idea of the direction of travel, but there were still some key points to settle.

We also didn't know how much longer the pandemic would be with us. As the month opened, the nation was enduring its second major wave of infections, with cases and death rates even higher than in the first wave. The vaccination program had begun, but serious questions remained around uptake, effectiveness, and the possibility of new COVID variants in the future.

Despite these uncertainties, several of the largest corporations in the US had begun to set out their plans for the post-pandemic workplace. The media picked up the subject and ran with it, starting a broader public debate that we couldn't ignore. It would have been nice to have time to dot all the *i's* and cross all the *t's*, but it was vital we kept our OneCausers in the loop while this discussion was taking place.

The prospect of writing about the plan was daunting. After all, changes in our work patterns would have dramatic effects on the lives of every member of our team. But the words of the Stoics (see Chapter 3) helped me focus my energies. I couldn't control the events in the world that were forcing my hand, but I *could* control how I responded to them. Even though the OneCause Future of Work plan wasn't complete, we knew what our priorities were, and we knew the principles that were guiding us. So I decided to share what we knew, what we didn't know, and our plans for filling in the gaps.

Writing this update wasn't easy. I had to balance a desire for information with the reality of where we were, and a positive vision of the future with honesty about the uncertainties ahead. That meant phrasing our plans very carefully to avoid creating unrealistic expectations, while also sharing the excitement I felt about the huge paradigm shift underway.

As had often been the case, the act of writing an update had unexpected benefits for me. Thinking about the language we used helped me think more clearly about our decisions and our goals. I included a humorous reference in the update to how we should probably stop using the word "remote," but in the months that followed I phased it out of my own usage.

"Remote" carries all sorts of baggage, suggesting distance from the center and people working far apart. I now make an effort to speak and think about *distributed* team members, people who are all in their proper place, wherever that place may be. While I still use the phrase "working from home," I am now conscious that this doesn't, and shouldn't, apply to all distributed staff. As we move out of the pandemic, people will increasingly fall into the "working from anywhere" category, with all the freedom and flexibility that implies.

Soon after writing the update, I made perhaps the most important change to my vocabulary: I stopped using the phrase "back to the office." When we are confronted with a moment of disruption as profound as the COVID pandemic, things sometimes change for good. If we seize the moment and use it to propel us forward, we have an opportunity to redefine our future. We can remake the world into something we could never have imagined before.

Sometimes, there is no going back. And that's something we should embrace. And so, we moved *forward* to the Future of Work.

February 13, 2021

future of work.

We're all starting to think about the same things:

- When are we going back to the office?
- Are we ever going back to the office?
- What will it look like?

Hey, I don't live in Indianapolis. I don't have an office to "go back to." What about me?

I just joined the company and I live out of town/state.
Back to the office:

- Will it be safe?
- Will I have to get a vaccine?
- Will everyone else have to get a vaccine?
- Will I be forced to come to the office?

As I previewed for you in our company meeting this week, we are embarking on a journey to answer most, if not all, these questions.

Here is the one thing you can count on—the future of work will NOT be the same as the "work" we knew and left on March 16, 2020.

I don't think any of us expected the transformational change that occurred in our work life. I found an email I sent in early May that indicated I expected to "return to the office" by June 14th. Ha!

If the impact of the pandemic would have lasted only a couple of months, I think it might have snapped back into its old shape. However (staying with the elasticity metaphor) the pandemic has so "stretched out" that there is no going back (kind of like the waistband of those sweatpants we've been wearing. ☺)

But, like some of the other COVID silver linings I laid out on Thursday, this may be a blessing.

Some of you may have seen announcements from tech and SaaS leaders like Facebook, Alphabet/Google, Amazon, Netflix, and Salesforce.

We will look to model some examples that are being announced and written about. We will also make some different choices.

According to a recent study by the commercial real estate firm JLL, 74% of employees still want the "ability to come into an office." Salesforce has indicated that number to be 80%. But workers still want the flexibility to NOT come in every day. We'll listen to that and make our plans accordingly.

The hard truth is that right now, as of this date February 13, 2021, COVID and its new variants still present a risk to our workforce. Despite daily good news about the vaccine, this risk still presents us with substantial uncertainty.

As I've previously indicated, through a combination of being "lucky and good," we have created a situation with tremendous flexibility. We're not committed to real estate. We don't have your typical five to seven-year lease.

So, with this flexibility in mind, we're able to shape our own vision of the "future of work." Here are some basic tenets that we will use as guiding lights for the decisions we will be making in the near future:

1. Ask our employees what they want.
2. Balance the needs of individuals, teams, and the business.
3. Be "People-first." Some positions will be "Office-first," some "Mobile-first," all will likely be "Hybrid."
4. The Indy office will serve as the "Hub" in a "Hub and Spoke" construct.
5. The Hub and Spoke construct will look more like a bicycle wheel than a steering wheel.
6. We will create a future of work that feels inclusive for the remote employees. We should probably stop using the word "remote." ☺
7. The role of the physical office will be that of:
   a. Collaboration
   b. Facilitating serendipitous "collisions"
   c. Teamwork and team meetings

      d.   Creativity

      e.   Mentorship

      f.   Learning

8. The layout of the physical office will be more: open.

9. The layout of the physical office will be less: a sea of desks.

10. For employees who are in the Indy area:

      a.   It will be rare for anyone to be required to be in the office five days a week.

      b.   It will be more common to be in the office two to four days a week.

      c.   We will work with the department leaders to determine the needs of the position.

As I said, we are embarking on a journey. We're getting some advice and guidance from professionals. I can assure you that our process will be:

- Thoughtful
- Considered
- Informed
- Thorough
- Inclusive
- Flexible

We're going to move forward with a phased approach. Here's how it might look:

1. Phase 0—Current state:

      a.   100% work from anywhere.

      b.   Base Camp is not generally available.

      c.   No real corporate HQ.

      d.   No "fear of missing out"—everyone is remote.

2. Phase I—New "Base Camp" office Open for business:
   a. Still basically work from anywhere.
   b. Base Camp starts to accommodate personal work and team meetings, with physically distanced workspaces, workroom, and two conference rooms.
3. Phase II—Phase I + co-working spaces (we're looking at various options around Base Camp).
4. Phase III—New plan for "work from anywhere" workforce:
   a. Work from anywhere vs. work from home as cities open up public spaces.
   b. Our plan will provide connection; inclusiveness; and support productivity.
5. Phase IV—New physical location for "OneCause HQ:"
   a. No earlier than the second half of 2021 or even early 2022—we have options.
   b. Hub and spoke model rather than fully distributed.
   c. Will need to be coordinated with Phase III for "work from anywhere" workforce to avoid FOMO.
   d. Will be purpose-designed and built for health and safety.
   e. Safety protocols will match those of the city and state.
   f. We will follow all guidelines for PPE, building access and occupancy, elevator limitations.
   g. In any event, we will consider the before COVID "office of March 2020" (B.C.) to be defunct.
   h. No one will be expected to come to the office five days/week.
   i. Non-dedicated shared workspaces.
   j. Think "laptop and backpack."
   k. Leave your plants and family photos at home.

I. Fixed monitors, workstations.

All of these plans will need to balance the needs of you as individuals with the needs of your departments and the overall needs of the business. Freedom and flexibility come with a mutual trust and openness.

We'll also have the opportunity to do things differently. We might be able to hire a more diverse workforce by removing geography as a barrier from filling certain positions. Reaffirming the OneCause culture with a work from anywhere employee base will require more creativity and imagination. We will stretch ourselves in new ways.

Reed Hastings, Netflix CEO, said the inability to get together in person is "pure negative:"

> WSJ: *Have you seen benefits from people working at home?*
>
> Mr. Hastings: *No. I don't see any positives. Not being able to get together in person, particularly internationally, is a pure negative.*

I don't agree with him.

As you can see, hear, and feel, there is a lot to consider. We have the opportunity to reimagine and reshape the "future of work" for OneCause. We will do this with thoughtfulness and purpose, and we will do this together.

"... *work is not somewhere you go, but something you do.*" —JLL research report

Thanks for taking this journey with me. Stay tuned. There's a lot more to come.

Keep your eye out for our first survey which will likely come out in the next couple of weeks. Let us know what you need.

We're listening. Until then, stay safe and healthy!

FEARLESS FUNDRAISING IN ACTION

In celebration of Black History Month, we want to shine a spotlight on causes honoring Black culture and contributions furthering social justice. Here's a look at just a few events and campaigns from our customers.

Emmett Till Foundation—Justice for Emmett Till Petition

The Emmett Till Foundation's mission is to bring truth, justice, and healing to the families of victims of unsolved murders committed during the civil rights era. Diana connected with their cause and donated a OneCause software subscription to support their efforts through our *Kickstart Your Cause* program.

With our Text2Give solution, the Emmett Till Foundation has been collecting petition signatures to bring long overdue justice for Emmett Till—who was tragically murdered at age 14 more than 65 years ago. To date, the petition has more than 15,200 signatures on its way to their 20,000 goal. You can still show your support by texting "Emmett" to 243725 to sign the organization's petition.

Our Place of New Trier—2021 Celebration of Black Culture

Our Place is a multi-year customer with subscriptions for Mobile Bidding, Peer-to-Peer, and the Virtual Fundraising Solution that supports teens and adults with intellectual and developmental disabilities. While we power the organization's Annual Benefit, golf outings, and peer-to-peer fundraising, this year they are truly taking advantage of the year-round value of our software, creating a special Giving Center site to celebrate Black Culture throughout February.

New content is added daily, honoring inspirational leaders in civil rights, government, sports, performing arts, fine arts, music, literature, and food. They also are encouraging their community to share ideas, experiences, etc. to contribute to the site. I encourage everyone to take a look at their resources to use in your personal celebration of Black History Month.

QUOTE OF THE WEEK

"We've worked with you guys many years and LOVE your services. Greatly appreciate you accommodating all our changing needs during the pandemic."

—Kenda, Director of Development, A Beacon of Hope Pregnancy and Relationship Resources

Let's go!

Steve

LEADERSHIP LESSONS

- **The problem with prediction**
  In crises, leaders need to balance forward-looking optimism with the sheer unpredictability of a chaotic future. There is a fine line to be walked between unrealistic certainty and leaving your organization adrift with no foundation for future planning.

- **Leverage the chaos**
  When a crisis takes everything you know and throws it into the air, the ensuing chaos offers opportunities. Look out for the unique moments to restructure our worlds that don't present themselves in times of stability. Create new frameworks from these new circumstances.

- **Be prepared to say goodbye**
  Sometimes a crisis can change things for good. When there is no going back, you can try to fight the tide or embrace the future and shape it. An important part of leadership is knowing when to say goodbye to old paradigms and look ahead to new frameworks.

- **Talking without telling**
  Sometimes as a leader, you'll find that you don't have all the answers, but you still need to communicate. The first step toward making that conversation meaningful is a radical commitment to honesty. Explain what you know and what you don't know. Proceed from there.

CHAPTER 11

The Fearless Journey

It was hard not to be conscious of March 2021 approaching. From the first day of the pandemic, we had all been measuring time, either looking ahead as we tried to guess when it would end or looking back at the lengthening road behind us. *"It's been almost a year now!"* was something I heard often in the first months of 2021. And then, here we were, in March again, COVID still with us. With 12 months behind us, the road ahead still stretched into the future with no end in sight.

The media, understandably, chose to mark the moment by counting cases, deaths, and recoveries, and by revisiting pivotal moments. This kind of memorialization is important. It's one of the ways we process hard times. It's how we weave our individual experiences into a shared cultural memory, a common reference point that links us together as a group. This communal storytelling takes place at the national level and in small towns, within families, and in cities. And, like any other community, it takes place at OneCause.

March 2021 gave me another reason to think about OneCause Nation's pandemic story: the TechPoint Mira Awards were approaching, and OneCause was a finalist in three categories. The TechPoint awards are an important date on the calendar for technology companies throughout Indiana, serving as a catalyst for the community by shining a light on achievements in the industry.

Over the years, OneCause (and BidPal, as we were previously known) has been nominated frequently and has won several awards. It's not why we do what we do, but it always feels great when our teams are acknowledged in this way. The 2021 categories included a special, one-time award for Pandemic Pivot of the Year, and we were very happy to be nominated and become a finalist.

When I began preparing our presentation, I saw an opportunity to do more than reel off facts and figures. I wanted to tell a story. Working on my updates each week had given me a fresh understanding of the different ways we use stories to make sense of the world around us. Each time I sat down at my keyboard, I knew that the tone I used, the information I chose to present, and the way I ordered that information would all impact the reader. The facts would remain the same, but by connecting them in different ways, I could tell very different stories about the same events.

The facts I had to work with were remarkable. OneCause had developed a new virtual streaming technology to help nonprofits connect to donors and continue fundraising in the pandemic.

We had helped raise half a billion dollars since the start of COVID, and our teams were doing everything they could to support our fearless fundraisers as they pivoted to keep their vital missions going.

And together we had lived through an experience unlike any other in our lifetimes.

I wanted to use the presentation to frame this journey. Of course, the first people to hear it would be the award's panel of judges. But before the first letter came up on my screen, I knew that my real audience was the OneCause team, the people who had traveled with me on this road.

Every message is improved when it is framed as a story. The "hero's journey" is a favorite narrative type of mine, and our pandemic pivot story was built around the heroes who had made it possible. The heroes in our tale were every single OneCauser who had risen to the occasion to help a customer or write a line of code and every parent who had adapted their home to balance work and family in ways never asked of them before.

The heroes were the nonprofits we worked with, the fearless fundraisers who leveraged the opportunities created by our pivot to make their own switch to virtual fundraising.

And the heroes were the donors who continued to dig deep and give generously as we entered an unprecedented period of economic uncertainty.

My role was that of narrator. I was in the fortunate position to give an overview of events from a perspective that might not have been available to those who were working at the sharp end. My goal was to pull together the threads and weave them into the storylines of hundreds of individuals into a single fabric.

This shared story could be told many ways. There was the disaster story, a tale in which crushing and unavoidable events sweep in to destroy our plans for the future, forcing us to rebuild from the ashes.

There was the gritty story of survival, of a team navigating through the unknown, pulling together against the odds to make it through to safety on the other side.

These stories resonated with me and would have had the audience on the edge of their seats. But they wouldn't have told the whole tale, or the whole truth of all those OneCausers who led our pivot.

From the earliest weeks, we had decided to seize the opportunity for positive change that the pandemic presented us. We had chosen to fight our way forward, setting out to redefine what was possible in our industry. Our story wasn't about reaching safety. It was about discovering a whole new world.

I wanted to look back, to set down a marker and commemorate the year that had passed. I wanted to take stock of where we stood today and what we had achieved on our journey. But I also wanted to acknowledge that our goal had been about so much more than just making it through the year.

Our pivot was a springboard, and where we stood now was just a jumping off point for the next chapter of our story. There were new challenges for the heroes to face, new battles to be fought. I wanted to tell the team, "This is *your* story. This is *our* story. The ending has not been written. What happens next is up to us. Starting right here. Starting right now."

March 13, 2021

one year later.

As COVID will be written into history books, March 11, 2020 may emerge as a date that will live in infamy alongside September 11, 2001 and December 7, 1941.

It's now been a year since that fateful day—and the surreal days that followed.

That said, it is remarkable that it has been "only" one year since the declaration by the World Health Organization of COVID as a Global Pandemic and the fact that now more than 101 million vaccines have been administered in the United States.

This is truly remarkable. I received my first "Pfizer" shot on Monday. I have to say that I drove away from IU North Hospital with a small feeling of inevitable victory.

"This is how it begins," I thought . . .

Among the 101 other things we were working on at OneCause this week, we presented to the Techpoint Mira Awards judges our case for the three awards we were nominated for. I presented our case for the *Pandemic Pivot of the Year* award. Stephanie and Tim presented our case for the Virtual Fundraising Solution as the *Product of the Year* as well as *Innovation of the Year*.

For my bi-weekly update I thought it would be worthwhile to reproduce for you my talk track for the Pandemic Pivot along with some selected slides from the presentation deck. A special thanks goes out to Karrie and her team for making these slides so spectacular as well.

My hope is that this will serve as a reminder of the amazing journey that we have been on together for the past year as well as something of an archive of the facts surrounding this time so that you can—remember.

Here it is:

Good morning. I'm Steve Johns, the CEO of OneCause.

I suppose that it's fitting that we are meeting on the 1 year anniversary of the WHO declaring COVID a Global Pandemic.

While it is a somber anniversary, we have great hope for this coming year for our business and for our customers.

Thanks for letting me tell you OneCause's story of leadership through our Pandemic Pivot.

When I was preparing to tell this story, I thought of the traditional story arc of a "hero's journey."

All good "hero's journeys" start with the protagonist in the known world and in a comfort zone.

The hero is called to action by a challenge or a need of some sort. We certainly face a challenge.

And this is what our world looked like:

Powering nonprofits to build better tomorrows

$4B RAISED *for* GOOD

MISSION
We help our customers connect with
more supporters and raise more money
by providing the best value in fundraising
software & support so they can focus on
advancing their mission.

10,000 NONPROFITS

40,000 FUNDRAISING CAMPAIGNS

2M DONORS REACHED ANNUALLY

Our origin story started in 2008 in Indianapolis.

Since that time, we've grown and scaled into one of the largest companies in our space.

We've won awards for innovation and growth and have been a 3-time nominee for Mira scale-up company of the year.

Our numbers supported it.

We were on a roll. We were stringing together multiple years of strong revenue growth.

We entered 2020 with a goal to help our nonprofit customers raise $1 BILLION.

We had every reason to believe in this.

BUT THE WORLD HAD OTHER PLANS.

On March 11th:

WHO declares COVID to be a global pandemic.

March 12th:

NBA suspends their season.

MLB cancels spring training.

NCAA cancels rest of the season including March Madness.

March 13th:

President Trump declares National Emergency and European Travel Ban.

I remember calling my exec team together on the afternoon of the 13th to talk about a game plan. Driving home that night, I thought, "This feels like the day after 9/11."

ON SATURDAY NIGHT MARCH 14TH THE TABLES WERE SET, BUT NO ONE CAME.

OVERNIGHT. We pivoted from nearly 100% in-person to nearly 100% virtual and online.

The CDC and other municipality guidelines restricted the number of people who can gather—from 250 to 100 and ultimately to 0—shelter in place.

THIS WAS OUR CHALLENGE. THIS WAS OUR CALL TO ACTION.

THE THREAT WAS EXISTENTIAL. TO US AND TO OUR CUS-TOMERS.

Fundraising Impact:

Planned in-person spring events—2,100

Executed in-person spring events—0

Compare this to the end of February and first 10 days of March, when we had powered over 300 events that raised $50 million.

Organizations that relied on these fundraisers to fund their annual operating budgets were in jeopardy.

This is the call to action that brought us from the comfort zone of the known world to the unknown and uncertain world we lived in for the rest of 2020.

When fundraising goes to ZERO in a moment, you have a choice.

Fight or flight.
We chose FIGHT.
We rallied around our call to "Fearless Fundraisers."

BEING **FEARLESS**

I N   A   T I M E   O F   F E A R

Put our "mask on first" . . .

- *Massive action to take care of our team.*
- *Ensure the continuation of OneCause.*
- *Expense rationalization.*
- *Cash planning.*
- *4-day work week.*
- *Reduction in discretionary expenses.*
- *Hiring freeze, travel suspended, and WFH.*
- *Full benefits, 401k match + add'l stock options.*

Led Largest Digital Pivot in History of Industry

- *Digital transformation similar to what we saw in online retail.*
- *We added 1,400 new customers between March and October.*
- *This is still playing out.*

Created a Vision for the New Normal

- *We defined what it meant to be Virtual first.*
- *We envisioned the future of fundraising and . . . .*
- *On March 23 we greenlit new product development on the Virtual Fundraising Solution.*

Enabled Nonprofits With Virtual Fundraising Solutions

- *Productized our Virtual Event Services and Virtual Event Manager in a matter of two weeks.*
- *Stood up the COVID Resource Center in the same time period.*

There was no playbook.

2020 Pivot Milestones

DEFINING VIRTUAL
- RELEASED VIRTUAL SERVICES
- LAUNCHED RESOURCE CENTER
- NEW INNOVATION BEGINS
- CLOSED HEADQUARTERS

FUNDRAISING IMPACT
- MULTIPLE SOLUTIONS
- CONTINUED FEATURE DEVELOPMENT
- NONPROFIT SUCCESS

MID MARCH — Q2 — Q3 — Q4

VIRTUAL TRIAGE
- TRANSITIONED FUNDRAISERS
- FORMED AGILE PRODUCT TEAM
- ALL-HANDS PIVOT MTG

EMBRACING VIRTUAL
- CUSTOMER PILOTS
- VIRTUAL COMPANY MTG
- OFFICIAL PRODUCT LAUNCH
- VIRTUAL RAISE CONFERENCE

There is no Board member who could say, "Based on my experience leading companies through global pandemics"...

We looked to the disaster recovery playbook of Response/Recovery/Mitigation/Preparedness and went to work...

Within days of the national lockdown we became "Virtual First," shifting our efforts to help nonprofits move fundraising activities online.

After putting our own masks on first, our priority became our customers who had scheduled fundraising events and were frozen on how to proceed.

Schoolhouse Rock presented by Cornerstone Schools of Alabama was our first transition from in-person to virtual. They pivoted in 24 hours and beat their pre-pandemic goals.

By Q2 we operationalized new virtual fundraising services, retraining our onsite event staff and consultants to support virtual events.

We recognized the market need and repurposed the talent we had, mobilizing our industry experts into virtual triage. These were our first responders.

We fast-tracked product development efforts to greenlight a new virtual fundraising solution. By July we were supporting pilot customers after condensing 18 to 24 months of development work into four, and officially releasing the Virtual Fundraising Solution on September 1.

All of this we were able to accomplish without a major reduction in workforce, ultimately making the strategic choice to leave our corporate office in May to invest the savings in retaining our people.

By Q3, we were running fully virtual events with embedded livestreaming for auctions and donations. Our annual conference for nonprofit professionals (Raise) experienced a surge in virtual registration to more than 7,000.

By the end of the year, our customers' fundraising proceeds were starting to meet or exceed comparable prior year months.

WE MADE A HUGE BET ON THE FUTURE AND BUILT THE VIRTUAL FUNDRAISING SOLUTION.

September 1—launched new Virtual Fundraising Solution—four months after whiteboard drawing!

- *More than a hundred subscriptions in first two weeks of product release.*

- *Nearly three hundred events to date.*
- *Tens of millions in fundraising proceeds on this platform alone!*
- *This is an integrated platform with a show manager for live-streaming, pre-recorded content, silent and live auctions, live appeal, donations, raffles, and chat—everything an in-person fundraising gala has.*

My colleagues are in another Zoom meeting right now presenting the Virtual Fundraising Solution for Product of the Year.

"OneCause has brought user-friendly donor and admin experiences to the virtual event space, with new and improved capabilities to help nonprofits accomplish all their goals," said Elaina, Director of Special Events for the Crohn's & Colitis Foundation New England Chapter.

"There just aren't other platforms out there that have all the key pieces you need to make a virtual event successful in one place, on one screen. Because of the Virtual Fundraising Solution, we were able to exceed our event fundraising goal helping to improve the lives of those living with Crohn's disease and ulcerative colitis."

[I then presented some stats on our Pandemic Pivot.]

BY THE NUMBERS
P A N D E M I C   P I V O T

9,392	76	96.6	25,000
EVENTS SUPPORTED	VIRTUAL SERVICES NPS	CUSTOMER SATISFACTION	NET NEW NAMES

44,000	115,000
WEBINAR REGISTRATIONS	COVID-19 RESOURCE CENTER SESSIONS

[I then presented two customer success stories representing two different perspectives of success—Avery Coonley School in the Chicago suburbs who was one of our first virtual events (in April) using our current auction and event software alongside Zoom streaming— and Crohn's and Colitis who piloted the Virtual Fundraising Solution in the summer and since then has executed 34 virtual events on the platform.]

IMPACT.

*These customer success stories are just two of the thousands of examples of nonprofit customers that we have helped pivot their fundraising through this pandemic. There is much I'd like you to take away from this presentation; but if you were to remember just one thing, it is this—**the impact** we made by choosing to fight.*

*Since March 14th 2020 and through the pandemic period until just yesterday, we have helped nonprofits raise nearly **$500 million** for their causes!*

This wasn't just our pandemic pivot. This was our customers and our entire industry.

*AND HOW DID **WE** DO?*

One team. OneCause. Expanded Workforce. Significant Software Growth.

Increased annual revenue and solid liquidity position forecasting growth in 2021.

We put our culture and our values first.

We stayed true to our core values of:

We are . . .

Passionate

Curious

Helpful

Committed

We made massive changes to our operating cost structure and got really lean. The entire team made an investment in our future. It paid off.

I committed to transparency and open communication with weekly updates as we made our way back and am happy to say I continue to fulfill that pledge.

We've been 100% WFH since March 16th with more than 300 employees in more than 30 states.

We accomplished all of this with a net GAIN in headcount over the past 12 months.

The future is very bright.

We've been recognized by the Indiana Chamber, (local) Powderkeg, and even Inc. Magazine for our steadfastness through this pivot.

In our hero's journey, we find ourselves having survived the test and returning to the known world.

But like every experience we go through, it has changed us permanently. For the better.

We are focused.

We are stronger having powered our way through the pandemic.

Our customer relationships are stronger for going through this together.

We learned to communicate. Be transparent. Be true to our values.

We are bullish for 2021.

I'd like to leave you with a quote by C.S. Lewis:

> *"You can't go back and change the beginning, but you CAN start where you are and change the ending!!"*

Thank you.

FEARLESS FUNDRAISING IN ACTION
United Way Elgin Middlesex—Sleepless in our City

In the past, Sleepless in our City participants slept in their cars as a symbolic gesture to help raise dollars and awareness for issues related to poverty and homelessness in the Elgin and Middlesex counties of Canada. This year, 22 DoGooders from across Middlesex and Elgin Counties stayed up all night, connected virtually from their homes, to raise dollars and awareness for local programs.

Throughout the night, participants took part in conversations with a lineup of local experts to learn about issues like hunger, mental health, intimate partner violence, and social isolation, diving deep into how each one of us can make a difference in our community, personally. Elgin County pulled ahead in the head-to-head fundraising challenge reaching 109% of their goal with Middlesex County quickly catching up at 97% of their goal with donations open until March 19th.

Make-A-Wish Central & Western North Carolina—Wish Ball

Two weeks ago, Make-A-Wish of Central & Western North Carolina hosted their first ever Virtual Wish Ball broadcasting live from Charlotte with auctioneer Ben Farrell hosting the evening alongside a special Wish Kid Co-host. Virtual supporters were encouraged to participate in the Wish Ball Dining, purchasing a meal from two area restaurants with 10% of the proceeds going back to Make-A-Wish.

The evening included virtual entertainment, inspiring stories from Wish Kids and their families, along with a successful live auction, silent auction, and Fund-A-Wish Appeal on our Virtual Fundraising Solution. Make-A-Wish reached 625 virtual supporters and raised funds to provide 80 Wish Kids with the life-changing experience of a wish.

QUOTE OF THE WEEK
Stop scrolling! ☺
This one is a long one, but definitely worth the read!

"I honestly cannot say ENOUGH about this software and the people who work at OneCause. Although I have used an auction software for eight years and have a fair amount of knowledge, I still think that this couldn't be easier. It's really amazing how well it works. The OneCause University is terrific. When I did get stuck on something, tech support was absolutely fantastic. The people are so kind—one woman essentially acted like a therapist for me the day before the event and pulled me off the ceiling."

"Truly, this was the best decision I've made about a software, and I've preached for a week about it. Although our event didn't raise as much as I would have liked, I can immediately even see what we could have done better the next time. Normally I would still be entering data without a hope of running credit cards for several days. I've already processed my payments and am DONE with the event other than thank you letters, etc. Anyway, it's fantastic, the people rock, and I'd do an advertisement for you I love it so much."

—Bridgid, Director or Development, Columbia Independent School

I know it was a long one, but I hope you enjoyed this update. This is *your* story.

Let's make it great!

Steve

LEADERSHIP LESSONS

- **Mark the milestones**

  Milestones are important, especially when navigating in a crisis. Commemorating progress helps to build culture by focusing on shared achievements. Past achievements also provide inspiration for those setting out on the next leg of the journey.

- **Balance optimism with realism**

  News of genuine progress is inspiring and can help make other goals feel attainable. Be sure to temper aspirational narratives with realism about ongoing challenges and uncertainties. The goal is hopefulness and optimism grounded in data, not empty optimism that ignores reality.

- **Stories have power**

  The way we tell our stories, both to others and to ourselves, shapes the way we view the world. By making the hero's story a shared story, we can create a common cultural narrative that unites teams and individuals around the goal of serving the customer.

CHAPTER 12

Keep on Moving

As OneCause marched into the spring of 2021, we could look back at our response to the first 12 months of the pandemic with pride. When our in-person events dropped to zero almost overnight, the OneCause Nation rose to the challenge. Instead of falling back, or even standing still, we pushed forward. We refocused the business on our new virtual and livestream solution, developed new capabilities for our customers to leverage our existing software, and adapted our working practices to the reality of the pandemic. Together, we fought every obstacle the virus threw at us.

But these achievements created a unique challenge, one that preoccupied my thoughts as the new year dawned: when a team has already achieved extraordinary things, how do you keep that momentum going?

In one sense, the answer was simple, follow through, to make the most of what we had already achieved, and keep progressing in an uncertain future. To do this, we'd have to "drive through the ball." I had used this sports metaphor in one of my first updates of 2021 to give an easily accessible visual image of our goal for the year. Instead of pulling back, we had to maintain the momentum of our swing and drive through the moment of contact. In baseball, it's that acceleration and focus that puts real power behind a player's efforts and ensures that the ball continues onward, to where they want it to go.

I liked that image of harnessing the past and extending it through to the future. I was trying to think ahead to where we wanted to be not just in 2021, but in 2022 and beyond. The metaphor of driving through, extending our achievements, felt like a good way of positioning ourselves for the long term.

Still, there was something this image didn't quite capture. While the ground-breaking development of several effective COVID vaccines gave us good reasons to feel optimistic, that optimism had to be tempered with reality. We still faced a huge amount of uncertainty moving forward. And that uncertainty raised questions: how do you drive through the ball when you aren't certain of the target? How do you prepare yourself for a race that has no discernible finish line?

The more I thought about it, I realized these were questions about life in general, not just the pandemic. Once COVID was finally gone, we might have more certainty about the short and the medium term, but the long-term future would always be an unknown. The future was the result of too many variables to calculate with any certainty.

That may sound scary, but it's actually a liberating way to think about the world. It means we have an amazing freedom to create our own futures instead of being forced down predictable paths. We *can* build better tomorrows because the tomorrows that lie ahead aren't already set in stone.

In November 2020, I sent out an update about the importance of treating every day as if it were "Day 1" on your journey (see Chapter 9). As we moved into the spring of 2021, that idea resonated more deeply. 2021 was a year of rebirth, a chance to live out experiences we had missed when the pandemic swept in the previous year.

Rebirth though doesn't have to be "one-and-done." We can choose to harness this fresh perspective and see every morning as a new beginning and every day as an opportunity to take a step forward. It's that momentum forward, that progress, that really matters, not where we eventually end up.

This kind of mindset can't be commanded or demanded from the "top" of an organization. Short-term targets and directions can be handed down through the lines of communication on a traditional org chart, but attitudes can't. The idea that the future is something to be created starts with the individuals that make up the whole. It grows from the base up, and that means every team member must become their own leader.

My job as CEO isn't to act as a drill instructor calling out the step. Instead, I want to empower and inspire every team member to lead themselves. This way, they can harness the creative energy that comes from choosing to take a new step forward every day, come what may.

Once you start marching forward with your eye on the horizon, it's not a final goal that matters. It's the rhythm, the cadence, the shared beat of progress as you step into the future together with the rest of the team. That rhythm can flex and change and adapt to uncertainty because it's not fixed. It can be created and recreated on the move, from minute to minute and hour to hour.

By putting our focus on progress rather than perfection, on the journey rather than the destination, we can draw on a bottomless well of momentum that is refreshed every single day.

January 15, 2021

drive through the ball.

If you've ever taken a golf or tennis lesson or received baseball hitting instruction, you've heard this refrain.

"You have to hit *through* the ball." What does that mean and why is it so important?

Think about not just hitting the ball that is there, but imagine that one or even two balls are coming in behind it and continue your swing through the initial point of impact. Accelerate through the zone.

As many coaches and hitting instructors will attest, hitting through the ball and following the angle of its incoming arc give you a better chance to drive the ball through impact. A follow through after that enables you to keep the momentum of your swing exploding through the ball without stopping.

OK, thanks for the completely irrelevant hitting lesson, Steve. ☺ Stay with me.

This week we completed our annual "Sales Kickoff" for 2021. The virtual meeting brought together sales and marketing and included presentations from other departments, a few of our fearless fundraisers, and outside consulting experts. *It was great!*

We said goodbye to 2020 and revealed our plans for 2021.

But as we talked about 2021, it made me think that we have to **"hit through"** 2021.

We need to make solid contact with 2021 and accelerate and follow through to 2022 and 2023.

2021 is not an end. 2021 is a point along our journey. We need to think and plan that way.

Everything will *NOT* go as planned. We know that for certain. But that doesn't mean we shouldn't plan.

If Abraham Lincoln really said this, then I am more in awe of him than ever:

"The best way to predict the future is to create it."
Abraham Lincoln

He was so ahead of his time.

So, as we look to the coming year, let's embrace and plan for its uncertainty. Let's take control of our future by planning and creating it. 2021 is our point of impact. Let's make good contact and drive through 2021 to the years ahead.

If you've ever played golf, tennis, baseball, or soccer you know how great it feels to make solid contact with smooth follow through. It keeps you coming back for more. ☺

Happy 2021!!

FEARLESS FUNDRAISING IN ACTION
U.S. Ski & Snowboard—Jeff Shiffrin Athlete Resiliency Fund

You may remember back in September I shared the launch of the Jeff Shiffrin Athlete Resiliency Fund to enable athletes to continue training during the unforeseen Beijing Olympics cancellation. It was Alpine skier Mikaela Shiffrin's personal story of loss and resilience that both inspired the fund and raised the awareness for the campaign through her interviews with the *New York Times*, CNN, and The Today Show.

Well, it was a big week for Mikaela as she achieved her 100th World Cup podium appearance, winning gold in the Women's Slalom on Tuesday, AND the campaign officially surpassed its goal. US Ski & Snowboard supporters from around the world (including 19 different countries, and 39 states) donated and shared their words of encouragement with Shiffrin and her teammates. Thanks to their donations and the notable donation match, US Ski & Snowboard will be able to support all 185 athletes pursuing their Olympic dreams in route to Beijing 2022.

Well, it's finally here. 2021. During the kickoff, I heard a few times the reference to "crushing" our goals for 2021. If you want to really see what "crushing" means, picture your favorite home run hitter, make solid contact with next year, and drive through to the years that are to follow.

This is the epitome of holding oneself to a higher standard. We need to "hit through" all that 2021 will throw at us and drive toward "crushing" our plan!

Here's to 2021 and beyond,

Steve

March 26, 2021

renewal.

Happy Spring 2021 OneCause Nation!

I love spring. There's something about the sights and sounds of *renewal.*

Of rebirth. Of coming back to life.

> Birds chirping.
> Tulips and daffodils peeking.
> Buds budding.
> Green grass poking.
> Grills grilling.

The smell of new mulch. Spring rain. Sunlight till 7 and later . . . ah, so nice.

While spring sprung last year in 2020, we didn't really get a chance to enjoy it. March 21st was simply the first Saturday of lockdown. The second Saturday of zero in-person events.

We were *"springing"* into action making sure that OneCause could sustain. We *sprung* into action to help our customers reschedule events or convert to virtual.

But we were being told to "shelter in place." Stay at home. Only go out for "essential trips." We were driving to Kroger, lining up, and loading up groceries. (Remember the substitutions? "We were out of ketchup, so we substituted some pickles." Cool? No, not cool.)

This really dawned on me while watching the opening days of the NCAA March Madness tourney. The announcers said it had been *"710 days"* since we had last seen the NCAA tournament.

That made me think, ". . . we really got cheated out of so much last year—but particularly spring."

All of those significant sports events that mark spring—March Madness, Opening Day, the Masters, Kentucky Derby—were either cancelled outright or "time-shifted" to later in the year sans fans. Your kids didn't get to go to prom, spring break, graduation, and other "coming of age" experiences.

So, this spring, we are making up for lost time. Sue and I went for a walk the other night, and everything felt so different. So alive. So fresh. So new. The buds were bigger, the daffodils were brighter, the grass was greener, the air smelled "springier."

Our renewal in 2021 is more than "spring." We are coming out of the grips of a year-long global pandemic. We see the light at the end of the tunnel, and it is daylight not an oncoming train!

Now is the time to renew.

Take stock. Spring clean. Rebirth.

It's only March 25th. If you haven't thought about this yet, it's not too late.

Do some of this to *set yourself up for success in 2021*:

Commit to be fit.
- Go get your annual health check. Establish your baseline.
- Set your goals.
  - Eat more this; eat less that; drink more this; drink less that.
  - My new thing is extra-virgin olive oil.
  - Target weight.
  - Find a partner and state your goal out loud to your partner. Ask them to hold you accountable. This works.

Simplify your workspace.
- Here's what I did. You will need a patient partner.
- Take everything off of your desk and put it somewhere (that's where the patient partner comes in) for short term storage.
- Now, only bring it back to your workspace as you need it. If you haven't brought it back to your workspace after a week or two, put it in long term storage.

Update your look for 2021.
- Hint, you're actually going out of the house this year!
- Stimulate the economy with that $1,400 check!

Get some rest.
- This year is going to be bonkers!
- Get your body ready for it.

Get your mind ready.
- If you haven't embraced mindfulness/meditation yet give it a try.
- Start the day with breathing. End the day with gratitude.
- Open up your complimentary subscription to the Calm app.

Get moving.
- Take a vacation.
- Take a long weekend.
- Run.
- Walk.
- Ride.
- Play catch. (Let me know if you need a partner for this!)
- Sit outside, close your eyes, and listen.
- Grill.

- Eat.
- Have a drink.
- Shoot hoops.
- Hike—we're discovering Indiana's fantastic state parks.
- Kayak.
- Play pickleball. ☺
- Reconnect with a friend.

We get to do all this again this year!

Look at this list. I feel better just writing it down. Go *do it*.

This spring is more than "spring." It's our awakening from the COVID Winter.

Make the most of it.

I'll leave you with this quote. Anne Bradstreet is considered to be one of our country's most important poets.

> *"If we had no winter, the **spring** would not be so pleasant:*
> *if we did not sometimes taste of adversity, prosperity*
> *would not be so welcome."*

> **—Anne Bradstreet**

Bam!

FEARLESS FUNDRAISING IN ACTION

Cornelia Connelly Center—Imagine Her Future

Cornelia Connelly Center (CCC) hosted their virtual benefit, Imagine Her Future, this month honoring alumni and CCC's mission to champion girls at risk with financial, academic, and social-emotional support from 4th grade through college graduation.

CCC leaned into their theme and each week leading up to the benefit featured a different student on social media sharing how they imagine their future. The event kicked off with a special pre-event Zoom conversation for VIP ticket holders followed by the Imagine Her Future broadcast and Live Auction led by student emcees. Top silent auction items included Career Coaching Classes, trip to Nassau Point and limited-edition art. At the end of the benefit, CCC surpassed their goal to help support their Middle School and Graduate Support Programs.

And now we're off to enjoy MLB's Opening Day 2021 on April 1st, and this year's bracket-busting March Madness, "March to the Final Four," culminating in the Championship game on Monday April 5th.

It finally feels like spring! ☺

With renewal,

Steve

April 23, 2021

progress not perfection.

"Perfection is the enemy of progress."

—Winston Churchill

Last night we were recognized with the **Pandemic Pivot of the Year** award in connection with the annual Mira Awards by Techpoint!!

It was an honor and a thrill to accept the award on your behalf! I will never forget it.

It was very special. It also came with mixed emotions. 2020 took a lot from us. With personal sacrifice, focus, and commitment we rose to the occasion and delivered for our customers. We kept them fundraising in the face of a global pandemic and helped them execute over 9,000 fundraising events generating over $500 million in proceeds.

This story has been told.

The story within the story was "getting stuff done." There's something about fighting for your life that takes you to a different level of performance. There's something about taking care of people you care about that allows you to endure so much more pain.

It requires action.

If you're too worried about making a mistake or failing, you'll never make progress. The pursuit of perfection can result in second-guessing and analysis paralysis.

We moved fast and broke things. Virtual Event Manager. Virtual Event Services. COVID Resource Center. Virtual Fundraising Solution. Virtual First. Hybrid.

We fought for our existence and defended our customers.

We didn't worry about getting it perfect. In fact, we know that we were NOT perfect.

However, we made progress!

We got stuff done.

Now, let's move on.

Now, as we move into the next phase, we have a new challenge. We need to keep that mindset! We need to keep high standards, we need to be excellent, but free ourselves from the pursuit of perfection.

We need to take that mindset and **impart it on our customers and prospects as well**. If not, we *and they* risk the consequences of:

- Procrastination
- Inertia
- Unrealistic standards
- Inaction

No progress.

On the contrary, the pursuit of excellence through learning, trying, and doing results in:

- Continuous improvement
- Growth
- Knowledge
- Learning
- Experience
- Meaningful change

Progress.

There's no way that I can express my full gratitude for everything that you all have done to keep OneCause strong.

However, we CAN commit to each other to keep it strong. You have mine.

Onward.

FEARLESS FUNDRAISING IN ACTION
Alonzo King LINES Ballet—2021 Gala

This year, the Alonzo King LINES Ballet rallied around a "There's No Standing Still" theme for their annual gala, hosting a virtual evening full of inspirational dance, conversation, and fundraising. The evening kicked off with an interactive pre-show where guests with VIP or Sponsor tickets could mingle with LINES Ballet's artists in virtual meeting rooms.

Tickets offered at different levels were available to receive a Celebration Box of treats and cocktails curated from Bay Area businesses and access to the pre-show event. The main show featured ballet footage, interviews from the Arizona desert, and special appearances by Debbie Allen, Mayor London Breed, Misty Copeland, and more. The generosity from 733 virtual supporters helped the organization surpass their goal and raise proceeds from ticket sales, sponsorships, live and silent auction, and a fund-a-need. The Gala received rave reviews in the *San Francisco Chronicle* too in an article titled: "Alonzo King Lines Ballet's spring gala offers hope for bursting 'COVID bubble'."

Here's to progress!

Steve

May 8, 2021

keep your eye on the horizon.

Is anyone else feeling a little unsettled? It seems that we are constantly tossed around by the events and circumstances of the day . . .

. . . making unbelievable progress with the vaccine rollout in the US.

offset by:

. . . the horrible situation with COVID in India.

then:

. . . the stock market (Dow and S&P 500) hitting record levels.

followed by:

... the live music/concert business continuing to delay reopening. (*Burning Man* cancelled again??!!)

And our business is seeing some of the same bobbing up and down:

... Hot leads are up! Hot leads are down.

... New business is up! Existing business is down.

... Existing business is up! New business is down.

... We're reopening! In-person fundraising is back!

... Not so fast! We're still virtual.

sea legs.

When you're on a ship in rough waters, your brain and body are disoriented. All the walking rules you learned and were programmed as a child are broken.

You can't count on the ground being solid for your balance. The "ground" is bobbing up and down, but also swaying side to side. As seagoers call it—pitching and swaying.

That does not feel cool. I know. I'm not so good on rough waters.

It takes a little while for you to get your "sea legs" under you.

What advice is given? My Uncle Jim loved to sail. He said:

"Keep your eye on the horizon."

Keeping your eye on the horizon gives your brain important information to help your body adapt to the ship's movement.

The other piece of advice that's given?

Don't go below deck or lay down. Keep standing.

Standing will continue to challenge your brain to reprogram as fast as possible. This won't happen if you're laying down or sitting down below deck. Keep standing.

If you fall, that's okay. Stand up and try it again.

Let's heed this advice.

In the ups and downs of our days, we need to **keep standing and keep our eye on the horizon.**

We need to be there for our fearless fundraisers. Their worlds are swaying, pitching, yawing, and surging too. Help them keep standing and keep their eyes on the horizon.

The rest of 2021 is going to be this way.

Let's get our sea legs.

FEARLESS FUNDRAISING IN ACTION
Well Aware—Shower Strike

For 13 years, Well Aware's Shower Strike has brought together advocates from around the world to raise awareness of global water issues. This unique campaign challenges participants to skip showers for a week (or until they reach their fundraising goal) to raise funds to build water projects in East Africa.

Well Aware provides options for participants to join in different ways, whether that's as an individual, company, or class/school pledging to skip showers, walk for water, or just fundraise their way. Sponsors play an important role by providing matching gifts at the beginning and close of the campaign and even join in on the fundraising action, including Spectrum Brands who created a mini employee competition with their own leaderboard.

The 217 shower strikers crushed their goal, raising impressive funds to bring clean water to more than 23,700 people.

QUOTE OF THE WEEK

"The overall support and personal interest made me feel at ease. Everyone was very helpful as well as pleasant and eager to make the event a success. There is nothing that you need to improve."

—Lisa, Founder & CEO, Hands That Make A Difference

Again this week, our customers and their creativity are showing the way! These customers are keeping their eye on the horizon. If you skipped through the Fundraising in Action section of the update, I'd like to encourage you to go back and read the "Shower Strike" success story.

Sarah Evans, the founder of Well Aware was a keynote speaker for Raise. They have created a unique way to focus on the importance of water (here in the US) to bring attention to the need for clean water in Africa. It's a remarkable story with remarkable impact.

These past couple of weeks were big! Record-setting event activity, board meeting, all-company meeting, and today my 34th wedding anniversary. ☺ (I had to get that in somehow!! Haha!)

As I said yesterday in our company meeting—we've come a long way, but we have a long way to go. Q1 got us off to a great start, but we have to keep looking to the horizon. Finish Q2 strong and prepare for the second half of '21. There's good momentum. I feel it. Let's seize it!

Keep standing and keep your eye on the horizon,

Steve

FEARLESS

LEADERSHIP LESSONS

- **Momentum comes from the ground up**
  Commitment to making progress can't be demanded by an organization's leaders. It's an attitude that comes from the ground up. The only real way to keep a team moving forward is to harness collective commitment and empower individuals to keep the momentum going themselves.

- **Your energy is a finite resource**
  Leaders at all levels, from the self-leading individual to the CEO, need to recognize that energy is a resource to be managed. Unsustainable short-term gains can lead to burnout if you don't manage your resources properly. To succeed in the long term, you have to know when to recharge.

- **Keep your eye on the horizon**
  In chaotic situations, the speed of change can be disorienting. A long-term perspective that looks to a future beyond the ups and downs of today can help you stay balanced when the maelstrom of current events is swirling around you.

CHAPTER 13

What Else Could This Mean?

2020 had been a continuous challenge for everyone, from the first dark days when COVID swept around the world, through the global shutdown, and then nine months that shook so many things we had taken for granted. Until the vaccine development program started to bear fruit, moments when we could truly feel optimistic were rare.

2021 took us down a different path: a roller-coaster that whipsawed us between hope and despair. Depending on where you turned and who you listened to, you could find visions of a reborn future or warnings of an apocalypse, often half a dozen times in a single day.

Those constant ups and downs were almost as hard to handle as 2020 had been. By the end of January, we had seen the vaccine rollout roar into action and a new COVID surge kickstart the deadliest wave of the pandemic. There had been an insurrection at the Capitol Building and the inauguration of a new president. We were posting historic stock market highs at the same time the data was describing the worst period in history for the economy. And that was just the first 30 days of the year!

That push and pull, the wave after wave of contradictory rapid-fire information, was enough to leave anyone disoriented. There was so much going on that it felt impossible to be fully informed. And, worse, all these shifts were happening on a macro-scale, beyond our control as individuals.

There was nothing that us "regular folk" could do to change any of these things. So how *could* we respond to this chaos?

When I wrote my update at the end of that tumultuous first month of the year, I wanted to share my own feelings about how overwhelming things could seem. I wanted to validate the worries of those across the OneCause Nation who were feeling the same way—stressed, tired, and even frenzied from the chaos. Most of all, I wanted to share some ideas about how we could respond to a world that seemed out of control.

Throughout 2020, I had written about the Stoics and their idea that we need to separate the things we can control from the things we can't. Once we've done that, we can let go of the latter and focus our attention on what is in our power. And the one thing we can *always* control is our own response to events. As we stepped into 2021, I wanted to focus on these responses as well as on the practical steps we could take to be healthy and happy.

The human brain is an incredible organ. It can perform complex calculations and create sublime works of art. It can feel love and sorrow, hope, and fear. It can design everything from Lego® models to whole societies. Yet one of the most amazing things our brains can do often happens without us noticing. Every second of every day, our brains construct the world we experience.

When we look around a room, the amount of information our senses pick up is vast. But instead of showing us every speck of dust in the air and every thread in the carpet, our brains have evolved to filter out less important things and focus on what matters.

Sometimes, that editing process doesn't quite work. We scan the hall looking for our keys, but our eyes pass over them again and again. It's only when we focus our attention on the side table that they stand out to us. The information was there all the time. Our brain was processing everything visible in the room, but what we actually "saw" depended on what we chose to pay attention to.

There's a lesson here for how we interact with the world. What we experience isn't just "out there" or "in here." It happens at the meeting point between the two. And while we can't change the world outside just by thinking, we *can* change our understanding and awareness of it. In a world that often feels like it's out of control, there's something liberating, something powerful, about realizing that we can shape the way we process things. We aren't victims. We're artists.

Every day, we use all sorts of tools to change the way we engage with the world. We get our caffeine fix in the morning because it will help us focus. We pick a quiet spot for thinking because it's easier to create or process ideas when we shut out distractions. We put music on to help us relax because the sounds and the rhythms make us feel a certain way. Whenever we take these simple actions, we are actively shaping our experience of what goes on inside and outside our heads.

Once we become conscious of this capability, we can start to engineer our responses to the world in an active way. We can take control of our feelings. We can direct our attention. And we can start to filter out overwhelming thoughts in the same way that our brains have evolved to filter out the thousands of pieces of sensory information that don't need our attention.

In my January 28, 2021 update, I described this filtering process as "stepping out of the waterfall," separating the endless stream of thoughts and media inputs from the "you" who makes the decisions. I'd made a similar point the previous month when I wrote about the Zen concept of *shoshin*, or "beginner's mind." This is the idea that we can choose to approach familiar subjects with the attitude of a learner encountering them for the first time. We can choose to see the world through fresh eyes, and this enables us to find new meaning in it.

FEARLESS

Underlying both these updates was the idea that helped me handle the ups and downs of 2021: *Meaning isn't given from the outside.* We can *choose* the meaning we find in events. We can construct it, and with it, our experience of the world. If events are getting us down or overwhelming us, we can always ask "What else could this mean?"

These weren't just abstract ideas. They were practical tools that helped me and our teams deal with some tough times, even if this perspective didn't always come naturally. When I wrote my update halfway through September 2021, I had to force myself to choose a different meaning.

September was frustrating for us. Every time it looked like we could start moving toward the post-pandemic era, a new variant would come along and knock our feet out from under us. OneCause had plans we wanted to put into action, goals we wanted to achieve, but events beyond our control kept throwing obstacles in our path.

At the same time, I felt let down that our country wasn't coming together in the way I would have hoped in the face of this challenge. Writing a few days after the anniversary of 9/11, I couldn't help but contrast our response to COVID with how we came together as a nation in 2001.

All that negativity poured out onto the page. I let my immediate feelings, my sense of anger, frustration, and disappointment decide what I wrote to the team. I failed to choose, failed to lead myself. I let my emotions take over instead of consciously choosing the path I took. When I read the draft back to myself, I was horrified. The words held nothing useful, nothing good or hopeful or inspiring. It was just a guy venting, blowing off some steam in a way that was no help to anyone else.

So, I deleted it. I stepped out of the waterfall, took a breath, and wrote an update that said something I thought was worth sharing. I chose what those events would mean to me, I picked the lesson I would walk away with, and I decided how I would respond. I changed my mind . . .

May 12, 2020

shoshin.

A few weeks back I encouraged you to "recharge." One of my suggested tactics was to re-engage in some reading of fiction. I used to read fiction a lot as I logged over 1 million miles on United alone. But for some reason, I got away from it.

I started reading a lot of business books—some good, some not so good. Even the good ones though didn't provide the pure escape of a good piece of fiction.

Well, I took my own advice. ☺ But rather than jump into the many options currently on the bestseller list, Oprah's, or Reese's list, I went straight to the Google machine and typed "Top 10 fiction books of all time." This yielded many results, most of which included these in some order:

1. *Pride and Prejudice*
2. *To Kill a Mockingbird*
3. *The Great Gatsby*
4. *Moby Dick*
5. *The Adventures of Huckleberry Finn*
6. *Brave New World*
7. *1984*
8. *The Catcher in the Rye*
9. *Atlas Shrugged*
10. *The Color Purple*

. . . and many others. What a list. I was hooked!

Of course, I have read many of these either in high school or college, but I wanted to experience them again (for the first time) with a *beginner's mind*.

"Shoshin" is a Zen Buddhist word which means beginner's mind. A beginner's mind is **"an attitude of openness, eagerness, and lack of preconceptions when studying a subject, even when studying at an advanced level, just as a beginner would."** (Wikipedia)

I ordered *The Great Gatsby* online to begin my journey. It was fantastic! I was transported to New York City and Long Island, circa 1922.

Hungry for more, I discovered another treasure—Black Dog Bookstore in downtown Zionsville! Black Dog is a used and rare bookstore—with actual books!! You can smell them, open them, and hear them creak, feel their pages, feel their weight.

As if it were the first time!!

I committed to buying hardcover versions of every book I was about to read.

I wanted the experience.

I followed Gatsby with *To Kill a Mockingbird* and then *Pride and Prejudice*. I'm currently reading Mary Shelley's *Frankenstein* and have *The Adventures of Huckleberry Finn* waiting for me.

"So much has been done, exclaimed the soul of Frankenstein—more, far more, will I achieve: treading in the steps already marked, I will **pioneer a new way, explore unknown** *powers, and unfold to the world the* **deepest mysteries** *of creation."*

—V. Frankenstein

This passage from Frankenstein also got me thinking about the beginner's mind. Studying a subject at an advanced level, but with an openness for exploration and lack of preconceptions!

My escape into fiction led me back to words of wisdom for OneCause. As we approach the end of the year and make plans for 2021, I want you to think with a beginner's mind (but of course, not trying to re-animate dead humans!).

A beginner's mind is:

- Free of preconceptions.
- Open to new experiences and adventures.
- Willing to learn.
- Filled with curiosity (one of our values!).
- Seeing things with "fresh eyes."

Think about the first time you really experienced:

- Wine tasting.
- Landing in a new city or country.
- Learning a new skill.
- Seeing a zebra, giraffe, gorilla, or leopard up close (it still boggles my mind).
- Eating exotic new foods.

On a micro basis, look at everything you do—setting your alarm, waking up, morning routine, the way you interact with your kids and your partner, how you manage your day, the foods you eat and what you drink, your night-time routine, and sleep patterns.

Starting today, look at each one of these tasks that have become routine with fresh eyes, new perspective, and an open mind to the experience. Truly notice—everything.

On a macro basis, look at your life. Really look at it. Truly notice—everything.

On a macro basis, look at your goals for next year. What do you want to accomplish personally and professionally? When you put the beginner's mind to work, you'll improve:

- Your relationships. You will pay attention to what you say and how you say it. How are you being perceived by others? Appreciate your colleagues and family. Appreciate your interactions with customers and prospects. Be open.
- Your experiences. Rather than going through the motions, you'll really experience and feel everything that you do. I know that I just want this year to be over. I just want COVID to go away. But that doesn't mean we shouldn't live every day and celebrate every day. Don't be frustrated with how you think things should be. Appreciate what is.
- What you worry about. Look forward to that next call with fresh eyes and a new perspective. What can you learn from it? How can you help someone today? Tackle that product development challenge with "beginner's mind" without preconceived notions about how it "should be done."

This message is for everyone. As we look to bring 2020 to a close, nothing magical is going to happen on New Year's Day 2021. COVID's not going away in a day. All of our customers aren't going to hold 500-person fundraising galas overnight.

So, let's approach 2021 with a beginner's mind. (It's a little like the "Day 1" concept I discussed earlier that Jeff Bezos preaches.) Let's see clearly what is right in front of us without preconceived notions. Let's open ourselves to the world of possibilities and curiosity that we had as a child and as we were first experiencing the world.

1. Let go of preconceptions.
2. Open yourself to new learning.
3. Give up on what you think "should" be.
4. Be open to new possibilities of what can be.
5. Ask questions.
6. Be curious.

"In the beginner's mind, there are many possibilities. In the expert's there is only one."

—Shunryū Suzuki

Welcome 2021 with a *beginner's mind,*

Steve

January 28, 2021

awareness.

Today, I turned down an invitation to a Pacers game for next week.

In the B.C. period (Before COVID), I used to look forward to a nice dinner downtown, walking over to Bankers Life, paying $15 for a beer, and cramming together with 18,344 other fans cheering on whomever happens to be wearing a Pacers jersey that year.

In the A.C. period—not just yet. But you have to hand it to the Pacers and the Bankers Life staff. I've filled out surveys, reviewed their new protocols, and seen the modifications they're making to their physical space. It is impressive. We're going to return. Soon. It will be different. Soon. But not yet.

This experience reminded me that no matter how we "feel" about COVID, the stark reality is that people are still testing positive, mostly recovering, but too many are still dying. We're all so sick and tired of being cooped up that we just want to DO something.

The media torrent is unrelenting. Virus variants, vaccine shortages, school openings, school teacher strikes, California opening, Governor recall count, GameStop Stock short mania, COVID cases down, but still 100,000 more could die, domestic terrorism. Apple has best quarter ever. Boeing has worst quarter ever. Tesla is up. Tesla is down. US worst economic growth since 1946. Dow, Nasdaq, and S&P 500 all in record territory, Impeachment 2.0, and on and on . . .

That doesn't even count what is actually happening to *us* every day. Our jobs. Our families. Our loved ones. Our friends. It can be overwhelming.

Our bodies and brains are barraged constantly every day. Over and over. Through social media, Slack, texts, emails, phone calls (mostly with bad news), and traditional media.

It is a torrent. We become caught up in our thoughts. They become a powerful waterfall.

I heard a great analogy last week that I'd like to share with you— compliments of my Calm app.

"Rather than being your thoughts and emotions,
be the awareness behind them."

—Eckhart Tolle

The analogy is that of a waterfall. If I had time and resources to create a waterfall graphic, the "waterfall" would include icons for Facebook, Twitter, Instagram, Slack, TV news, *The New York Times*, *Wall Street Journal*, gossip, kids, relationships, finances, new cars, old cars, mortgages, rent, health, safety, frustration, anger, disappointment, sadness, anxiety, joy, happiness, fulfillment, passion, courage, tenacity, resilience, grit, and on and on. It is a *torrent* of inputs, emotions, and thoughts.

YOU have to STEP OUT of the waterfall.

The Calm app went on to tell me, *"Cultivating mindfulness is stepping out of the waterfall and getting a different vantage point."*

Hey, I'm just a preacher's son from a working-class town. We didn't talk much about mindfulness or awareness in the '60s and '70s when I was growing up.

"Huh?" "Mindfulness?" "What?" "Awareness?"

I'm learning here right along with you and trying to share my own realizations with you the best I can.

But this made so much SENSE to me!!

I was already doing it. I just didn't know it.

Anyone who has worked on a project or presentation with me knows that my process starts with getting up and finding another space to sit. I can't do it at my desk in front of my laptop. There are too many distractions. The waterfall of the day is torrenting right in front of me.

I get up and go to my circular table in my office. I find a couch or comfy chair. I get up and walk. I start my process with a stack of plain white printer paper and begin to create!

I STEP OUT of the waterfall of my day and get a different vantage point.

To paraphrase the experts, we spend so much time thinking about things that we tie up the resources we need to actually observe our own thoughts and understand why we are thinking in a certain way. Have you ever said, *"I'm too close to this issue."*

Or, *"Let's get up to 30,000 feet so we can really see what the issue is"* or someone is *"not seeing the forest for the trees."*

We become immersed in the torrent of thoughts, emotions, and inputs of our day and become swept up and almost drowned by it all.

Find a physical space to create this awareness of separation. Find a chair, a pillow, a mat, a quiet corner, the bathroom if you have to!! Use that physical separation to try to separate your mind from the inputs of the day and *observe* with objectivity.

It's really important to quiet this torrent right before we go to bed. How'd you like to dream your Facebook feed all night? Or run through the headlines of the day blaring from your TV news.

As I was writing this, I thought about the current book I'm reading—*Brave New World* by Aldous Huxley. In this future dystopian society set in AF 632 (After Ford), babies are created in test tube bottles and when "decanted" are moved from the "Hatchery" to the "Baby Nursery." Here they are "fed" social and moral rules and lessons while they sleep—known as "hypnopaedia" conditioning.

Delta children are conditioned to **hate books** and Alpha and Beta children learn that "even Epsilons are useful."

Haha! Crazy right?!

Yes indeed.

But you still get the point. Disconnect. Hours before you plan to go to sleep.

STEP OUT from the waterfall. Give yourself a different vantage point. A different perspective.

A different relationship with and to your thoughts. Separate "you" from your thoughts so that you can look at your thoughts and go *"Wow, I can't believe I was having those thoughts or emotions. They are so unhealthy."* Then you can begin.

This is awareness.

FEARLESS FUNDRAISING IN ACTION
Church World Services—CROP Hunger Walk
Church World Services is one of our newest peer-to-peer customers, but very well known in the industry as their CROP Hunger Walk has often been called "the granddaddy of charity walks." In December, CWS launched their 2021 CROP Hunger Walk site on

OneCause Peer-to-Peer, seeding it with beta tester participants and teams who were still actively fundraising in 2020.

The homepage of their peer-to-peer site features a map with details for all the local walks across the US and a national leaderboard tracking activity across all walks. On January 9th, they officially opened registration for spring CROP Hunger Walks and last week hosted a webinar to tour the NEW "crophungerwalk.org" site (aka their OneCause Peer-to-Peer website). To date, 851 individuals and 261 teams have registered and are actively fundraising. We can't wait to see their impact and reach in 2021!

I'm looking forward to working together with you in '21 to make it our best year ever!

With awareness,

Steve

September 14, 2021
what else could this mean?

I deleted my first version of this update this weekend.
    I wrote it, read it, and decided to delete it.
    You see, it was too negative. I was letting my frustration get the better of me. It was not worthy of a leader.

On these days that we are remembering the sacrifices of the heroes of 9/11 and how our country came together, I was frustrated and embarrassed by the behavior of our country today.

And I wrote about it. And it just got me more frustrated. It wasn't productive for you or me.

So, I followed my own guidance and reminded myself that,

> "We can't control the events and circumstances of
> life around us, but we can control how we react."

There are so many versions of that quote going around that I'm not attributing it to anyone, but its origins do trace back to our old friends the Stoics.

Epictetus said, "It's not what happens to you, but how you react to it that matters."

He also said, "You become what you give your attention to."

I certainly DO NOT want to become part of the negative spin cycle of today!

So, I for one am asking the question that I led with—"What else could this mean?"—and taking control of how I react to the situation.

When we ask that question, it opens up a whole range of possibilities that "break the pattern" of negative thinking associated with the issue.

By controlling the meaning internally, you can shape the outside outcome.

Rather than getting emotionally charged that someone is attempting to purposefully sabotage our future ask, "What else could this mean?"

So whether it's fighting over masks, vaccinations, the withdrawal from Afghanistan, the next Greek letter COVID variant, or the validity of Bitcoin and meme stocks—take a breath.

Pause and ask, "*What else could this mean?*" and take control of the outcome!

It's hard. I know. But, I'm going to try harder.

You with me?

FEARLESS FUNDRAISING IN ACTION

Make-A-Wish Foundation of OKI—Indianapolis Hope is Essential Gala

Last month Make-A-Wish Ohio, Kentucky, & Indiana hosted their biggest fundraising celebration of the year—the Indianapolis Hope is Essential Gala. Guests who joined in person were able to safely enjoy dinner and drinks, bid on exciting live and silent auction items, rock out to live entertainment from Groovesmash, hear inspiring wish stories, and help bring hope, strength, and joy to children around Indianapolis through the power of granting wishes.

Those who were unable or uncomfortable to attend in person were offered a seamless virtual gala experience. With the generosity of over 900 supporters, Make-A-Wish OKI saw stellar silent and live auction proceeds and impressive donations for their worthy cause. Even better—the OneCause team was able to show their support while working the event!

QUOTE OF THE WEEK

"I felt very supported by my OneCause support staff. They all were readily available to help whenever I needed them and go above and beyond in ensuring that our event was a success. I cannot thank the

team enough for their support and for answering all of my questions as this was my first time navigating through this platform."

—Annie, Logistics & Operations Coordinator, San Francisco 49ers Foundation

Remember to ask, "what else could this mean" and take control of the outcome!

Steve

December 5, 2021

perspective.

As I reported last week, I spent some time in Florida over the Thanksgiving Holiday. I watched the sun rise yesterday. But, then again, I didn't. The sun didn't rise.

The Earth rotated. It really depends on your perspective.

As the sun continued to "rise" above the horizon, I let myself see it from a different perspective. If you've ever watched the sun rise over the ocean, it actually moves surprisingly quickly. As I let myself see that occurrence from the perspective of the earth rotating on its axis, I actually *felt a little disoriented*. A little wobbly. Just for a moment. Hey, we're moving!!

A little research revealed that we're actually rotating at 1,000 MPH! And, in case you're not dizzy yet, while we're rotating on our axis, the earth is hurtling around the sun at 67,000 MPH!!

See things from a different perspective. See how that feels.

Stephen Covey said, "*Seek first to understand then to be understood.*"

Abraham Lincoln said, "*Judge not, for you would do the same thing if you were in that position.*"

Elvis said, "*Before you abuse, criticize, and accuse, walk a mile in my shoes.*" ☺

Understanding another perspective brings me around to one of our core values. We are . . . **curious**.

Being curious requires you to be a "perspective seeker." Literally none of us come from the same background nor do we possess the same perspective. My brothers and I grew up in the same household, but we couldn't be more different in our perspective. My kids, the same.

Yet here we are at OneCause. More than 300 unique individuals who share a common vision. A shared purpose and mission. We have 300+ different perspectives helping almost 10,000 customers—each of whom contains many differing perspectives.

If you can do the exponential math, that's A LOT of differences. How in the world does anything get done??!!

We recognize and appreciate the differences in perspective and therefore in people.

We seek diversity in perspective and make ourselves better.

We recognize that our own perspective is just that. Our perspective—and then we allow ourselves to see things from another's vantage point. Another perspective.

Then, we unite around a common goal. Our common purpose and vision.

We stay committed to the goal but flexible in our approach.

This isn't easy. In fact, it's really hard. Seek a different perspective to...

> ... learn something new.
>
> ... see something known in a new light.
>
> ... leave "room to be wrong."
>
> ... understand that you might *not* have been wrong, but just saw things differently.
>
> ... see that there might be more than one "right" answer (not binary—right and wrong).
>
> ... create optionality.
>
> ... strengthen relationships with yourself and others.

Now, as we hurtle at unimaginable (and undetectable) speeds around the sun, let's get a new perspective.

Open up. Be curious. Seek out someone else's opinion. Be humble enough for understanding.

Then, share yours.

As we bring 2021 to a close, it's important to keep it in perspective. It wasn't the breakout, return to full in-person fundraising year that we hoped for—but to our credit, we did not plan for it. 2021 began with dark days in January and February followed by the positive news and momentum of an available vaccine in the late spring and into June. Then the Delta variant emerged to create headwinds for the second half.

All in all, and with proper perspective, 2021 was a solid year. Together with our customers, we emerged from 2020 with increased commitment to fundraise—virtual, online, peer-to-peer, in-person, golf, and galas—we did it all!

Now, we're ready to take on 2022! How will 2022 look? What's your perspective?

Drop me a note . . .

FEARLESS FUNDRAISING IN ACTION

Erin's House for Grieving Children—OneCause Friendsgiving

Q: How do you make a great product even better? A: Exercise.

On Thursday, November 18th, 2021, OneCause Nation came together for a luncheon to enjoy gourmet pizza and Affy Tapple caramel apples and to celebrate Friendsgiving. The assignment was to exercise the Virtual Fundraising Solution. Together, we did just that, providing the product team with valuable feedback to help refine the evolving virtual solution and ready our all-new OneCause Fundraising Platform for 2022 launch.

But in classic OneCause fashion, we did more, raising more than $3,000 for our customer, Erin's House for Grieving Children. It was a sold-out, in-person experience leveraging the latest and greatest features available for both in-person and virtual attend-ees. OneCause Nation rose to the assignment by participating in a program showcasing silent and live auctions, donation appeal, silent auction, and fixed priced items.

We're in the home stretch. Just a few more weeks and it's "Happy New Year 2022!"

Seeking perspective,

Steve

LEADERSHIP LESSONS

- **We're artists, not victims**

  We can't control everything that goes on in the world, but we *can* control how we respond. The ability to create meaning and choose what we make of our experiences, how we react, and how we move forward is the source of all creativity.

- **Cognitive diversity matters**

  In managing an organization, avoiding groupthink lays the foundation for creative problem solving. The more different perspectives and life experiences you can bring to bear on a problem, the more options you will have to select from when you choose a solution.

- **Engineering change**

  Editing your perspective can be a valuable part of the creative process. Choosing to look at your subject matter from a different angle lets you see it afresh and draws your attention to new features. Curating your environment can also lead to changes in mindset and sources of new ideas.

- **Lead holistically**

  Modern leadership isn't just about getting more out of your team in the workplace. It's about making sure they are engaged and being supported as a whole person, in their whole lives. It's about providing opportunities for their creativity to flourish.

CHAPTER 14

Time

Times change. Sometimes we forget this during periods of stability. We get used to routine and regularity, everything happening to a predictable schedule. But wait long enough, and the seasons turn: fashions become uncool, trend lines flip, and innovation reshapes the world. The pandemic has been an important reminder of just how much and how quickly times can change. But it has also been a reminder that time itself isn't the fixed and immutable background to our day that it seems to be.

It was almost impossible not to become interested in time as COVID took hold. Every day, the media overflowed with talk about units of time: cases per day, annualized mortality rates, and the weeks between the peaks and valleys of each wave. We counted the hours until we could leave our homes and hug our friends again. We counted the months until the first vaccines would be ready. We counted anything that might mark progress towards a return to normality. Time *mattered*.

And it wasn't just the units of time that were important. The way we experienced time shifted. Sometimes, when I look back over the last two years, it's all a blur, a rapid-fire sequence of huge events that shot past, the one fading into the next. Momentous days faded into the distance as the next big headline loomed. And the next . . . and the next . . . and the next!

The shift was driven in part by the significance of events. Few people experienced a lazy, relaxed, uneventful year in 2020. Too much was happening, often too much to track. And when time did stretch out, it wasn't like the hazy days of teenage summers that seemed to last forever. For many people, it was the sense of time stretched thin: anxiety, worry, and seemingly endless waits to fulfill basic human and social needs, like meeting family members face to face or having a meal with friends.

In a way, the pandemic cut us adrift from our normal experience of time by taking away many of the markers we rely on. Large parts of the framework that defined time simply disappeared. We lost the clear demarcations of leaving home in the morning, spending time in the office, and then returning in the afternoon or evening. Parents lost the time when the kids were at school, and they had the house to themselves. Weekends became just an extension of the week, as we passed the time confined to our bubbles. We had to rebuild schedules, seek new significance, and redesign our lives to fit the strange times we were living in.

Time was often on my mind, and I came back to this theme repeatedly in my updates throughout 2021. I wanted to talk about how we could best use the time we have (continuing a theme from 2020, see Chapter 6). As well, my updates were an opportunity for me to reflect on the complexity of how we experience and think about time.

Shifts in the way we experienced time could be unnerving, but I wanted to find something positive in them. The fact that it was possible to experience time in different ways was a jumping off point for me. If time isn't just something going on "out there," that means *we* are involved in creating the experience. And if that's the case, what can we do to take control of that experience and make it meaningful for us?

One of the most important factors that changes how I experience time is purpose. Purpose is what gives time meaning, what makes it significant. When I'm doing something meaningful, time never drags. I don't watch the clock, just waiting for the moment I can punch out.

Instead, time glides past in a smooth flow that, if anything, shoots by too quickly.

I've been the CEO of OneCause for nearly as long as I've been in any one spot in my life. But that time doesn't weigh on me. This job has a meaning that is unique in my career, and as a result, every day feels fresh, important, and full of purpose. We're lucky that what we do at OneCause makes it easy to find meaning in our work. But the decision to see that meaning—to focus on it and allow it to shape our experiences—that's a choice we have to make.

Early in October, my update shared an ancient Greek concept of time with my fellow OneCausers. The Greeks distinguished "Chronos," the measured ticking away of time in its succession of units from "Kairos," those special moments when that ticking clock stops, and you become completely absorbed in what you're doing. These treasured Kairos moments come from being absorbed in an instant, but they aren't just things that happen to us. We can act to help create them for ourselves by seeking meaning in what we do, by finding our purpose and allowing ourselves to be swept up by it.

There's something else the idea of Kairos time can teach us. Kairos isn't just about being in the moment. It's also about grasping the *opportune* moment, those instances of opportunity when you have a chance to make a real difference in life. For the Greeks, these moments were so important that Kairos was worshiped as a god.

The most famous statue of Kairos shows him with a long lock of hair hanging down over his face. His head is shaved bald at the back. This unusual image was a visual reminder that you have to seize your moment as it approaches you because there's nothing left to grab onto once it has passed. There's a lesson for all of us in that simple truth. Regardless of our job and personal situation, we all have the same number of hours each day. Those minutes and hours race past, but we can all choose to seize the moments as they come. We can make a conscious decision to take the opportunities that present themselves and make them meaningful. If we adopt the mindset that what we are doing matters, we find meaning in every minute. All we have to do is reach out and grasp it.

September 27, 2021

net positive.

For anyone who has heard my personal "Why" or journey to OneCause, you know that it all started with a magazine article. That particular article was found in the December 2013 issue of *Wired* magazine featuring interviews with Bill Gates and Bill Clinton. (I still have my original copy in my office.)

Clinton and Gates were discussing how they were leveraging their successes in their "first careers" to help "fix the world" in this next phase of their life.

I was doing some beach reading and had my moment of realization. Bam! That was it. My lightning-strike moment. I set my magazine down on the sand and looked at my wife. "That's it!"

I lacked Purpose. Mission. Meaning. I had a great career, but I was feeling empty and unfulfilled. I was still searching, but I didn't know for what or why.

I wasn't doing anything to add to the "good of society." I searched, and I was found!!

Then, a few years later (I know I've told this story before, but bear with me . . .), I was celebrating yet another birthday with my extended family, and my mother-in-law (we have the same birthday!) asked me, "*How do you feel turning . . . , Steve?*"

I said, "*You know what Peg? I feel great! I feel great because for the first time in my life, I can honestly say that the world is a better place for me being here.*"

I mean I'm a good dad, a good husband, and a pretty good friend, but I had never been able to quantify the "good" I was doing quite like being the CEO of OneCause.

Last week I was taking some time off to "sharpen my saw" and another magazine headline caught my eye. It was this headline on the latest issue of *Harvard Business Review*—"*Is the world better because your company is in it?*"—"The Net Positive Manifesto" by Paul Polman and Andrew Winston.

Well, "*Yes it is, thank you,*" I thought, but let's learn more . . .

The article begins by making sweeping statements that really resonated with me.

In this world of COVID, social injustice, depletion of natural resources, natural disasters, divisiveness, and more . . .

"*For their own good, companies must play an active role in solving some of our biggest shared challenges. The economy won't thrive unless people and the planet are thriving.*"

And if you know me, you know that this is not about altruism. I'm always looking for economic benefit. So, they went on . . .

"*. . . success was not at odds with financial performance; in fact, it drove profits and growth.*"

The authors used the term "*net positive*" to describe this way of unleashing the power of people, technology, and financial resources to build long-term shareholder value by serving the greater needs of the world.

One of the authors, Paul Polman is the former CEO of Unilever, named for 11 years in a row at the top of the world's leaders in sustainable growth.

There's some good stuff in here. It's worth a read. Like every-thing I read and recommend, don't take everything they say as "gospel." Take what you need. Take what makes sense to you. Then, take inspiration and take action.

I want people to know that the world is at least a little bit bet-ter because OneCause is in it. We do so much good now, but we can do so much more. We need to continue to challenge ourselves every day to look at how we do business, who we do business with, and the impact we are making on society, making sure that it is a **net positive**. So, read along with me and get inspired to take action.

Stay tuned for more here. I'm not done with this topic . . .

FEARLESS FUNDRAISING IN ACTION
Boys & Girls Clubs of Bellevue—Great Futures Day 2021
The Boys & Girls Clubs of Bellevue launched its Great Futures Day this Wednesday, a one-day unifying fundraising event that brings together the BGCB's community of donors, partners, volunteers, and friends to raise critical funds for their local Clubs.

The organization recruited 58 Great Futures Day Ambassadors to help spread awareness and raise donations toward their goal. The week leading up to the giving day, BGCB executed a social media blitz building excitement for the campaign with videos from volunteers, leadership, and benefiting children.

The record-breaking giving day was a huge success ensuring all 15 Clubs can continue providing the resources and support local youth needs to navigate these uncertain times.

As we look to the future, we need to recognize our place in this world and our responsibility to make it better because we're in it. We can make those better tomorrows while still creating shareholder value.

You with me??!!

Staying net positive,

Steve

October 9, 2021

time.

Lately I've been thinking a lot about time. This month I'm celebrating my seventh (7th) year as CEO of OneCause. Where did that time go?

I actually started on Monday September 29, 2014, but for some reason my start date is officially listed in October.

I know you know what I mean when I say, *"Sometimes that feels like just yesterday, and sometimes if feels like forever ago."*

Just for kicks I went looking in my old emails and found names like: Katie, Rich, Rachel, Will, Karrie, Dan, Kris, and James.

A smile came to my face ☺ as I read "welcome" emails and remembered the issues of those times.

Seems like forever ago. But it was "just" seven years ago.

Often time flies and other times it drags on.

We've now endured a year-and-a-half (18 months) of COVID. 21% of my OneCause career has been spent in COVID.

Seems like forever.

I've written about this in the past. I might have even said, *"Time is a feeling."* Isn't that true?

I recently learned, courtesy of my Calm app, that the ancient Greeks had two different names to capture this feeling. The Greek word for time as it relates to time as measured by a clock is "Chronos." But the word that refers to time as more of a moment or a feeling is "Kairos."

Everyone recognizes Chronos from its use in words like chronometer and chronograph to measure time. Chronos is quantitative. Chronos is how time moves slowly.

Chronos is deadlines and deliverables. Working against time.

Kairos on the other hand was used to express that special "moment" when time disappeared. You were lost in your moment. Time stands still. We've all had them.

A mountain waterfall suddenly visible from around the bend.

A quiet forest with leaves falling all around you.

The birth of a child.

Love at first sight.

The glow of 4th of July fireworks on the faces of your children.

A moment of great accomplishment in your career, sport, or relationship.

Kairos moments are qualitative, not quantitative. It's also referred to as the "right time" or the "opportune time." It's measured in experiences.

"In Kairos that part of us which is not consumed in the burning is wholly awake."
Madeleine L'Engle

We lose track of Chronos time with Kairos moments.

Our shared mission at OneCause has provided all of us with so much opportunity for Kairos moments in these past seven years:

- Getting through that first tough year in 2015!
- Completely changing the business and raising fresh capital in 2016!
- New leadership in 2017!
- Rebranding to OneCause and acquiring Great Feats in 2018!
- Massive scaling with National accounts, Inside sales, Resellers, and more in 2019!
- More new leadership in 2020!
- The thrill of recognition from the Mira Awards and *Inc. Magazine* for our virtual pivot in 2020!
- Year after year taking Raise to the highest levels of thought leadership!
- The tears of joy from smashing fundraising goals with our customers!
- The thank you notes from grateful customers for our people!
- Getting back to the ballroom in 2021!
- Raising hundreds of millions of dollars for thousands of customers and their causes!

The amazing people, products and processes that have contributed to grow OneCause from what it was in 2014 to what it is today and what it is poised to become in 2022 and beyond.

That's how you spend seven years in Kairos time. ☺ Seems like it went pretty fast. Yikes!

You can't go looking for or manufacture Kairos moments, but you can know what you are looking for and be able to stop and enjoy them along the way.

Put yourself out there. Take a risk. Challenge yourself. Give yourself more chances.

Reap the rewards.

Recognize and enjoy your moments. Give yourself a gift.

Live your life in Kairos time.

FEARLESS FUNDRAISING IN ACTION
Riverview Elementary PTA—Annual Parents' Night Out

We had another in-person pilot last month, helping create an engaging fundraising experience for the Riverview Elementary PTA (and our very own Dani) at their 4th Annual Parents' Night Out event. This annual event brings together parents for a fun evening of food, libations, and fundraising for the PTA & Leader in Me program.

Supporters were encouraged to wear their favorite jersey and school colors as they participated in tailgating and sports related activities, including the memorable tug of war. VIP tickets were also sold for early entry, exclusive access to the VIP tent, and branded Riverview Elementary swag.

Virtual tickets were available for access to the silent auction, featuring unique family and teacher experiences. This was a good opportunity to continue testing in-person functionality including check-in, check-out, and mobile bidding while helping to raise money to support the PTA's remarkable efforts.

Fall is a great season for Kairos moments. Pause to enjoy the warming sunshine that will be replaced by winter chill. Take a moment to enjoy the leaves as they turn from green to red, yellow and brown, and ultimately fall to the ground replaced by snow and ice.

Enjoy the last month of baseball and the beginning of football from high school "Friday night lights" to Sunday afternoons rooting for your team and taking a well-deserved nap.

There's a smell in the air. A feeling. Take a moment to let it wash over you.

Breathe it in.

Live in Kairos time,

Steve

December 20, 2021
past. present. planning.

Mindfulness teaches us to "be present." Being present is about taking the time to appreciate what is happening right here, right now without replaying the past or getting caught up in planning for the future.

While I certainly subscribe to this approach as a tool for mindfulness and calm, I can't help but feel the conflict with 1) learning from the lessons of the past, and 2) planning for the future.

You know that I'm a "gratitude guy," and we have to look to the past as well as the future for our gratitude list. I'm also a planner. To-do lists and goal-setting are a regular part of my repertoire. How could I create a compelling vision for the future if I am only "being present?"

We just submitted our budget for 2022 to the Board for approval. Houston, we have a budget!

Something tells me though that I don't think our Board would have appreciated it if your CFO and I would have said, "... *Hey, let's not dwell in the past, and let's not get caught up worrying about the future; let's just be present.*" Very Zen, but not very practical. Haha. ☺

How do we manage this apparent conflict?

I hope some of you have been able to download and use our new benefit to support your mental health and wellness—the Calm app. It's well-documented in this update that I'm a fan.

I've set out to balance this conflict by seeking wisdom from past "Daily Calms" as well as other teachings—including this famous Chicagoan:

> "*Life moves pretty fast. If you don't stop and look around once in a while, you could miss it.*"
>
> —*Ferris Bueller*

What I've learned is that we can truly achieve this balance. First, we must master the degree to which we engage in these thoughts. It's really a lot like everything in life—everything in moderation. If we "dwell" in the past or allow ourselves to "get caught up in it" or "consumed" by it, we're in trouble. If we can apply a discipline of moderation and simply be "inspired" and "informed" by it, we can still be present.

By the same token, if we can apply the discipline of moderation to our future, we can avoid being "consumed" or "overwhelmed" by it. We can be driven to succeed today (present) by the vision of the future we have crafted for ourselves.

So, let's use mindfulness and the art of "being present" to be the bridge between past and future. (I'm really making this up as I go, and I'm not sure Zen teaches this, but stay with me. I think

I'm onto something. ☺) As you sit each morning or each evening, reach back into the past for inspiration, learning, and motivation. But don't stay there too long.

Wordsworth said:

> *"Life is divided into three terms - that which was, which is, and which will be. Let us learn from the past to profit by the present, and from the present to live better in the future."*
> William Wordsworth

A word about "being present."

Acknowledging the past and planning for the future should NOT in any way diminish "being present."

Being present is so important. Just ask Ferris. Being present means:

- Pausing to reflect.
- Taking time to enjoy life in the moment.
- Giving yourself a break.
- Just being.
- Stilling your mind.
- *Really* listening during a conversation (practice this over the holidays).
- Enjoying the food you (or someone you know) took the time to prepare.

Being present is not laziness, being lackadaisical, or uncaring about the past, or planning for the future. Being present is taking the time to pause and reflect. Living in the moment. Today.

It's with this reflection that we can adequately set about planning our future. We have to have a solid foundation upon which to build, or our plans and execution will collapse.

We're coming up on the time of year for reflection (the holidays) and planning (the New Year). We're also being bombarded by continued negative news about the spread of COVID—now through the Omicron variant—21 months after it first began to impact us. It will soon be two years.

We don't know what 2022 will have in store for us. Let's reflect on the lessons of the past, appreciate today, and plan for a better tomorrow.

I choose to believe that 2022 will indeed be better. I'll see you next year. ☺

FEARLESS FUNDRAISING IN ACTION
Urban League of Metropolitan Seattle—Era of Essential Service

A well-thought-out breakfast program sponsored by Amazon, Microsoft, and several other big brand names, set the stage for a virtual affair hosted by Urban League of Metropolitan Seattle. Virtual guests joined the 20th Annual Breakfast: Era of Essential Service at 8:30 AM PT to reflect and reaffirm Urban League's mission to create a strong and prosperous community.

The OneCause Virtual Fundraising Solution provided engagement for 240 virtual guests who chatted the morning away, viewed extensive live and pre-recorded broadcasts, received perfectly timed messaging, played the sponsorship mini-game, and rose to the call to action.

Urban League of Metropolitan Seattle raised impressive funds to carry on with their five pillars of focus: advocacy and civic engagement, education, housing, public health, and workforce development.

As 2021 comes to a close, and we look forward to 2022, *I'll be coming to you monthly.* I'll generally time my updates to the second or third week of the month so that I can have final numbers for fundraising proceeds and events.

As the Delta and Omicron variants have proven, we are not yet in the "post-COVID" period. However, as you will see from our 2021 results which we'll report to you in February, we're on our way to growth again.

For now, I wish you all the very best for a safe and healthy holiday and New Year. It's with tremendous gratitude to all of you for what you do every day that I say, "Thank you for a great 2021, and see you in the New Year."

Looking to the past, present and future,

Steve

LEADERSHIP LESSONS

- **Meaning matters**
  We lead ourselves most effectively when we shape our actions to achieve meaningful ends. Meaningful goals create moments of joy in their completion and satisfaction in their pursuit. By using our time to do things that matter, we not only work better, we experience a higher quality of life.

- **Time is hybrid**

  The time we experience occurs where our perception meets the world outside our heads. It is a product of how we think and feel as much as it is marked by the ticking of a clock. If we harness our control over the experience of time, we can tap into one of the most important creative resources available to us.

- **Don't be passive with time**

  Time isn't just something that happens "out there." *We* can shape time and determine how we experience it, so it's important to make the most of what we have available to us. Purpose, intention, and seizing on opportune moments give our time meaning and significance, both as individuals and as teams.

CHAPTER 15

Connect

OneCause is a business built around connection. We build technology that leverages the connective power of computers, mobile devices, and the internet. We connect donors with nonprofits so they can connect with the causes they support. But OneCause is also a network of human connections, an extended family that brings individuals together as parts of a greater whole. We couldn't do what we do if our team members worked in isolation. We rely on each other for friendship, inspiration, ideas, support, shared resources, and so much more. It's the human connections that make us who we are: OneCause Nation.

One of the greatest losses we all endured in the pandemic was the sudden stripping away of so many opportunities to connect. At OneCause and throughout the country, our lives turned upside down overnight. For the first time, we were told that we had to stop connecting in the ways that were most familiar and dear to us. In this strange new world, closeness and physical proximity were suddenly threats.

Across America, the results were profound. In addition to the fractured connections caused by more than a million deaths, the number of those experiencing loneliness and isolation soared. For some, the effect was short-lived. For others, the experience of staying at home and being detached from wider family and friendship groups meant anxiety, depression, or worse.

I was in the privileged position of working from a comfortable home shared with a loving and forgiving partner. As the CEO of OneCause, I could also shape my work interactions in a way that wasn't available to everyone. Yet as the weeks and months passed, I still felt a deep sense of loss at the connections we were all missing.

Connection isn't just an optional extra; it's a fundamental human need.

Research in psychology and neuroscience has shown that loneliness and social disconnection lead to negative health outcomes, while the feeling of being connected with others and of belonging to groups has the opposite effect. Feeling connected not only improves our well-being and long-term mental health, but also correlates with better physical health and even a higher life expectancy.

Human connections aren't just life affirming—they're life preserving! They are a vital source of meaning and happiness, and connections make life worth celebrating.

One of the reasons my updates became so important to me was that they gave me a way to stay connected with the wider OneCause Nation. When I sat down to write, it wasn't just one-way communication. Instead, I was responding to things I had heard and learned in the previous weeks, reflecting on what was important to other members of the team, thinking about how I could be helpful or encouraging or share something that might inspire someone.

The updates gave me an opportunity to link myself to other OneCausers, to put myself in their shoes and try to see the world through their eyes. They acted as a tether that kept me connected to our community.

That sense of still being part of this amazing group despite the physical distance and social dislocation kept me going through the darkest times. But I also used my updates to reflect on the importance of friends, family, and staying connected with a life outside work. I wanted every OneCauser to focus on their health and well-being as a whole person, to draw on all the resources available to them.

It wasn't always easy to find meaningful ways to interact when we weren't allowed to be in the same room with the people we love. But the urge to overcome those barriers—to find new ways to connect and hold friendships and families together—has been one of the most inspiring revelations of the last two years.

The experience of physically reconnecting with my OneCause family in the summer of 2021 was momentous. After a lot of careful thought about case counts, risk levels, and personal comfort, we finally got together as a whole company that July. It was the first time we had all been in the same location since the pandemic began.

Talking face to face with people I hadn't seen since the start of the pandemic, and meeting many of our newer team members in person for the first time, was exhilarating. The high stayed with me for days after! I was so inspired by the event that my update at the start of August was twice as long as usual, and longer than any other I sent out that year.

I wanted to encourage everyone to take hold of that moment and use it as a catalyst to reaffirm old connections and forge new ones. The key message I wanted to share, both here and in later updates, was, "Commit yourself to reconnecting!" When the pandemic had done so much to take connections away from us, we needed to reclaim them, not just as OneCause Nation but as human beings.

My connection to my family has always given meaning to my work by grounding it in the goal of keeping them happy, healthy, and secure. OneCause is family too. The closeness of the connections and the intensity of the bonds may be a little different, but our OneCause Nation is much more than just a bunch of people getting paid to do a job. We are defined by the way we connect with our customers and make their causes our own. Every OneCauser is part of a community with shared goals, shared values, and a shared dedication to our fearless fundraisers. And it is in pursuing those goals and living those values that our work finds its meaning.

July 2, 2021
family.

I decided to take my own good advice and take a little time to recharge. With the coming 4th of July holiday break, we made plans to take a family driving trip to explore some of the sites that have long been ignored in favor of more exotic destinations.

And yes, my "kids" are not kids at all, but at 30 and 27; they decided to make the trip with us.

Now, you might have visions of Clark Griswold and the "family truckster" and you wouldn't be too far off. Packed sandwiches, water bottles, grapes (provide both food and drink!), chips, cheese and crackers for eight hours a day ☺—with a little Wall Drug just for fun, haha!!

There's nothing like driving across the western plains together to remind you of what is truly important:

- Family.

You're reminded of:

- Why you do what you do.
- Why you really do what you do.
- What you've invested your entire life in and for.
- Your legacy.

- How your kids have picked up some of your habits—and they are truly annoying.
- How your kids have picked up some really great learnings along the way too.
- Sibling rivalry is still a thing.
- Fierce family competition on game night.
- There's nothing you wouldn't do for these people.
- How funny, smart, and great your kids have become.
- How different their views are from yours.
- What it takes to navigate those differences with love and respect.

Family.

Shopify CEO Tobias Lütke recently made headlines for declaring that Shopify *"like any other for-profit company, is not a family. The very idea is preposterous. You are born into a family. You never choose it, and they can't un-family you."*

He went on to say that Shopify is more like a "team" than a family.

For all the reasons I cited above, I respectfully consider OneCause to be a family. An extended family, but a family, nonetheless. I routinely "welcome" our new hires to the OneCause *family.* I do this unabashedly and unapologetically.

When people decide to move on, I tell them, "You will always have a place you can call home."

Another phrase that I have learned to share with my kids is this, "I disagree with you, but I respect your right to your opinion. That's why this country is so great!"

As a OneCause family:

- We will disagree.
- We will find a way forward together.

- We rely and depend on each other.
- We are working together toward a common goal/legacy.
- We spend more time together than we do with our "first family."
- We recognize the talents and contributions of our family members.
- We engage in friendly competition. But if threatened, we defend each other.
- We invest in each other for that common goal/legacy.
- We support each other.
- We treat each other with care and respect.

OneCause Family. Team OneCause. OneCause Nation.

I want to wish each and every one of you a very happy and safe Independence Day holiday. We live in a great country that only came about through the personal sacrifice of those who came before us.

We owe it to them and to our families to make the most of it.

We're also turning the page on the first half of our comeback year. As I've said before, get ready for an explosive (catch the fireworks reference?) second half!!

You are my extended family. And guess what? Because this country is so great, you can disagree with me. If you want.

That's OK.

So now as we take time with our first families (away from our OneCause family) please pause, reflect, and recharge. Remember who is most important and why you do what you do.

Happy 4th of July/Independence Day!

Steve

August 1, 2021

human connection.

There aren't enough words to express the emotions most of us felt last week. Almost 200 of us gathered in-person for the first time as "OneCause Nation" since July 2019—two years ago.

> *For those of you who attended virtually due to concerns about your health or the health of loved ones you are responsible for, please continue to take care, and I look forward to seeing you again very soon!*

For those who gathered, many of us had never met in person. Until then, some of you had never even met your manager or your teammates in person! That would have been unheard of in the past. But *this is now.*

Sure, we had some fear and trepidation in our initial greetings. We didn't want to overstep our teammates' boundaries. We wanted to show respect for that personal space we had been "social distancing" from for so long.

Tuesday was a cautious, feeling-out day. Are you wearing a green, yellow, or red wrist band? (Good call, marketing team.) Should I Handshake? Hug? High five? Fist bump? Elbow bump? Wave? Nod?

(Personal note: I found that the fist bump became my go-to fav.)

On Tuesday we also honored nine teammates celebrating their 10-year anniversaries with OneCause! If you're new to OneCause or if you're just **curious**, reach out to one of them and ask them what it's like? See what you can learn about **commitment** from these **passionate** veterans!

For reference and posterity, they are: Dan G., Dawn L., Emily N., Josh M., Katie T., Kelly V.H., Kurt M., Nicole T., and Rick S.

Wow! Talk about the faces on Mt. OneCause! On a personal note I'd like to add my own thanks and gratitude for all their years of service to our customers and for helping to pave the path for those who come after.

By Wednesday afternoon we were drenched in sweat from the Indiana heat and humidity—high-fiving, jousting, hoop shooting, three-leg and sack racing, and obstacle-coursing in a team competition at White River State Park.

We were bonding through competition. Establishing new relationships and strengthening old ones. We were finding out that that person who we couldn't find a way to connect with over Zoom is actually pretty cool. Maybe we can find a way to work together. Maybe we can reach a compromise on that issue.

Human connection. *In a world of algorithms, hashtags, and followers, know the true importance of human connection.*

We also found out that the engineering team (particularly, Peer Factor) can kick butt! We were reconnecting outside of Zoom calls, but also outside of office walls, conference rooms, and stand-ups.

We were getting a big dose of human connection.

> *"Deep human connection is...the purpose and the result of a meaningful life - and it will inspire the most amazing acts of love, generosity, and humanity."*
> Melinda Gates

We came together as humans and laughed, cried, and told stories of our shared experiences. We celebrated past victories and commiserated over past hardships.

Scientists have studied the power of the human connection for years. There are scientific studies (and we are following science these days, right?) which have shown that human connection can reduce the stress hormone *cortisol* and may also lower blood pressure. One long-term study I read even indicated that human connection can be as impactful on your long-term health as avoiding excess alcohol consumption or smoking.

It might also be true that human connection creates something of a positive feedback loop. People who feel more connected feel better both mentally and physically, present more confidently, and experience less anxiety and/or stress. This creates something of a loop of social, emotional, and physical well-being. (Not an exact science of course, but it makes sense, doesn't it?)

If that's true, then the opposite is also unfortunately true. The absence of human connection leads to loneliness, feelings of isolation, anxiety, and a decline in mental wellness. I know that a number of us have experienced some of these feelings during our extended COVID lockdown.

Going back to science, there are also studies that show a lack of connectedness (i.e., isolation or loneliness) can take a toll on you physically including on your brain and heart, and even cause inflammation throughout your body.

Human connection.

> *"We are hardwired to connect with others, it's what gives purpose and meaning to our lives, and without it there is suffering."*
> Brené Brown

So where do we go from here?

I was told by MANY of you, *"Steve, this was exactly what I needed"* and *"This was perfect timing"* and *"We **all** needed this."*

Has the following ever happened to you? It's happened to me:

You've gone to a camp, a retreat, or a seminar and had a break-through. *You're going to change*!! But you return home and start getting comfortable again and engaging in the same destructive behaviors that were revealed to you and which you vowed to stop!

Don't lose the magic of what you just experienced! If you're geographically distributed from your team, ask your leadership if you can get together more often in smaller groups—maybe quarterly. Schedule a get-together around an upcoming conference or customer visit.

If you're here in Indy, connect more. Keep it going. Challenge another team to Top Golf or "Fowling" (pronounced like "bowling", which is some cross between football and bowling)—ask around. ☺

Connect it with problem-solving, ideation, planning, doing a retro on past projects.

Be mindful, and we can find it in the budget.

Make it fun. Make it about maintaining the human connection.

"But what about the Delta variant, Steve?" "I don't feel comfort-able yet."

That's cool. I know a lot has been said and written about the "Delta variant" and the new "breakthrough infections" to the vacci-nated. Please moderate your activities to your comfort level. We're still in the unknown. We all have different thresholds.

Return to human connection with your OneCause family as you feel comfortable.

But use last week as a catalyst for change.

human connection.

FEARLESS FUNDRAISING IN ACTION

United Healthcare Children's Foundation—Century Ride

The United Healthcare Children's Foundation hosted its 10th Annual Century Ride this past month. The UHCCF Century Ride was started by several committed leaders from the UnitedHealth Group now deemed "The Original Eight" who auctioned off their time to participate in a 30-mile cycling ride within the Minneapolis area.

The annual event has grown to a 100-mile cycle along the shores of Lake Minnetonka. This year, virtual riders were able to join in from their own locations. This year's campaign also spotlighted four child Grant Ambassadors sharing first-hand the impact of a UHCCF grant. A passionate group of 188 participants and 17 teams joined the fundraising effort with the top fundraising team of 12 raising remarkable funds.

In total, the 10th anniversary ride surpassed its goal for UHCCF medical grants.

QUOTE OF THE WEEK

"Working with Stefanie was fantastic. She was organized, detail oriented, and was so helpful in the weeks leading up to the Golf Outing. Jennifer and Jill were both onsite at our outing and were incredible day of. The set-up process and training of how to use the tablets were excellent. They both made the check in process go so smoothly which I was incredibly thankful for."

—Kim, Director, Fundraising Campaigns & Volunteer Engagement (Special Events) Crohn's & Colitis Foundation, Illinois Carol Fisher Chapter

We're all united in our common vision. Our Cause. While we commit ourselves to carrying that cause into the second half of 2021, remember to connect with each other. It's the human connection that gives us our reason. Our shared purpose to **help** our customers raise more and connect more to advance their mission(s).

To better tomorrows,

Steve

October 24, 2021
friendship.

I just got back from a wedding this weekend. The daughter of a longtime friend, business partner, colleague, boss, and mentor got married on Friday night.

It was the first time since March 2020 that we had seen so many of our friends. They represented couples we had spent weeks vacationing with, friends we had worked with for decades, and kids our kids grew up with. They know us. They've seen us at our best... and our worst.

Friends.

I haven't written about friends in a bit. Even when we weren't locked down by government order or simply too afraid to go to a restaurant, bar, club, or show, it was hard to maintain friendships. We're all so dang busy with our own stuff.

We have Facebook after all, right? *"Steve, I have friends. I have 656 of them. I know where they went on vacation, when their birthday is, and I even 'liked' what they had for dinner last night!"*

We all know how silly that is.

Next week, I'm going to my 40th high school reunion. That's right. My 40th! Class of '81 baby!! My high school friends "like" my infrequent postings on social media. They send me birthday greetings. I send them birthday greetings.

But do we *really* know each other in the way we did back in high school? So much has happened since then that we're different people now. Reconnect with old friends.

During the past 18 months, our friendship circles have changed. We retreated to COVID "pods" of safety and like-mindedness. Or your "pod" may have been determined by proximity or family.

In any event, we changed the way we gathered. The way we made and maintained friendships.

According to one research firm, Unacast, which analyzed GPS data from millions of cellphones, Americans gathered in groups 80 percent less than we did before the pandemic.

Seeing these old friends again reminded me of how very special friendships are.

Friends show up for you. Friends have your back. Friends would do anything for you. The support of friends helps to increase your sense of belonging and purpose. Friends shoot straight. Friends tell you, you have something in your teeth. ☺ They help you deal with loss and amplify your joy.

Some studies have even indicated that good friendships might help you live longer.

Friends are chosen by you, not by birth.

So, as we look to the COVID-present and to the COVID-future, I want you to think about friendship. Think about those friends with whom you might have lost touch. Those friends who really know you. Those friends who would do anything for you. But those friends who for some reason you may have lost touch with.

Stop and think right now and write down their names. Every time I start a new notebook, I start it with carrying over the names of those I want to make sure to connect with. I don't always accomplish my goal. But that doesn't mean I should stop trying. It just means that I wasn't committed enough to that goal to make it happen.

Commit yourself to reconnecting.

Put yourself out there. Be the first person to reach out. Don't wait for a call—make the call (or email or text). Let your friends know that you're ready to see them whenever they're ready.

We're still navigating here, let's do it with our friends.

For this update, I'll leave you with this from E.B. White's *Charlotte's Web*:

> *"Why did you do all this for me?" he asked. "I don't deserve it. I've never done anything for you."*

> *"You have been my **friend**," replied Charlotte.*
> **"That in itself is a tremendous thing."**

FEARLESS FUNDRAISING IN ACTION
Cooperative for Education—Fall Fiesta 2021
This past weekend, Cooperative for Education hosted a special Fall Fiesta livestream event on our Virtual Fundraising Solution, encouraging supporters to host a watch party with friends and family. This year's event featured a silent auction with unique trips and

experiences including a New Year's Eve in Las Vegas, virtual burrito dinner with Ryan Van Duzer, and local Cincinnati staycation and dining activities. In addition to the auction, Cooperative for Education sold out all its fixed-priced donation opportunities including a luxury raffle for an Orlando vacation, 10 mystery gifts, and sponsorship of six Rise students.

The Fall Fiesta 2021 was a great success, raising funds to break the cycle of poverty in Guatemala through education programs.

Make-A-Wish Foundation of San Diego—WINE & WISHES 2021
After having to postpone their 2020 event, the Make-A-Wish Foundation of San Diego's Annual Wine & Wishes event came back this past weekend for an in-person celebration again from a safe outdoor venue under the stars.

Tickets sold out fast, as the event reached capacity with additional supporters joining the virtual auction access. Four hundred supporters gathered for the in-person event experience, enjoying a selection of wines from Napa Valley and Sonoma winemakers, artisanal tequila and Mezcal tastings, and a program showcasing wishes granted through music, movement, and dance.

Giving through ticket sales, silent and live auctions, raffles, and donation appeal raised significant funds to support local wish children—17% more than they did at their 2019 event!

That's all for this update.

In friendship,

Steve

November 9, 2021

celebrate life.

My dad is the oldest of 7 siblings. He's 87 and living a good life. He's "happy and healthy," say his caregivers.

He has dementia.

He celebrates life every day. You've never met anyone happier or who could put a smile on your face so readily. He doesn't know how to make a phone call or write a letter anymore.

He still celebrates life every day with a smile.

My uncle Ted was 82. He battled Parkinson's. He just lost that battle.

I'm on my way to Surprise, AZ for a "Celebration of Life" for my Uncle Ted. He was an incredible "gentle giant" of a man with beautiful kids (my cousins) and grandkids. When asked how we was doing, he'd always reply, *"I'm just fine,"* followed by, *"But how are YOU?"* He was suffering so much, but he never wanted it to be about him.

He celebrated life.

Unfortunately, we know that the next couple of years are going to bring more of the same for the siblings in my extended family.

I come from a heritage of Lutheran pastors. My grandfather, dad, and three uncles are/were all Lutheran pastors. In good Lutheran tradition, we'll sing songs, hold hands, and talk about a "better place."

But for right now, let's celebrate life! Right here. Right now.

Don't wait until you "retire," 'cause what is that anyway?

Don't wait until you can "afford it." Hint: you never will.

Don't wait until the kids are "older," "out of school," or "grown." Hey, it's too late then. [Google *"Cat's in the Cradle"* by Harry Chapin and you'll know what I mean. Right, Boomers?]

Don't wait.

Celebrate life now!

Uncle Ted and my dad have lived very full lives. They're lucky to have hit their middle 80s and seen their kids married; grandkids born, graduated from college, and making their own way in life.

Not everyone gets that chance. As I told you last update, I went to my 40th high school reunion last week. Amid the revelry, we stopped and toasted to "those who were no longer with us."

Don't wait. Nothing is guaranteed.

This past year and a half has changed us. We're reassessing everything. Our relationships, how we work, where we work, our purpose, and how we balance and prioritize it all. Folks are retiring early, quitting their jobs, and pursuing new careers.

Throughout our country, this emerging phenomenon is being called the Great Resignation.

I'm referring to it as the Great Reassessment.

I'm encouraging you to take stock. Reassess. Take stock of your life—in all things:

- Career
- Financial
- Mind
- Body
- Soul/Spiritual
- Health
- Relationships
- Adventure
- Fun

If you don't like something, commit to changing it. Write down three actions you could take today to create lasting change in your life.

Remember, it's not what happens to you that matters, it's the actions you take in response.

If we can help, let your manager or me know. Let's face it. Look at the list. We're never going to be a "10 out of 10" on every facet of our lives at every moment in our lives. But we should commit to having a plan to get there. Achieve some balance along the way.

Let's take stock and celebrate life together.

Why? Because we're about to embark upon what could be the most exciting and important time for OneCause since its founding.

And you're here at this moment in time with me making it happen.

2022 will be filled with positive change. The OneCause Fundraising Platform and Peer-to-Peer Fundraising Software will represent the beginning of the next generation in fundraising solutions for OneCause and our customers. It will ultimately not only be the home for fundraising, but also for data and analytics, supporter communications, integrations, and so much more!

We're changing the where, how, when, and why we work with the "**Future of Work**" plan. This plan will be people-first, flexible and balanced to provide for continued impact from your work for our customers and amongst your team, balanced with the new needs of the Great Reassessment.

And finally, I expect **generosity** as a whole to break out in 2022. The pandemic year of 2020 saw giving increase in total in the US, but event-giving declined because people were prohibited from gathering. 2021 came back a bit but was hampered by the Delta variant. We enter 2022 with a record number of fundraising subscribers/customers/nonprofits whose donor base finds themselves wealthier with growing stock portfolios, wage inflation, and unprecedented savings from the lockdown and stimulus checks. The Great Reopening was delayed a little, but it will be unleashed in 2022. Just look at a stock like Live Nation to see what investors think about that!

I'm now writing this to you on Tuesday morning. I've been swept up in the activities of the days. That's only served to solidify my message to you.

Celebrate life. Today and every day. Don't wait.

In memory of Ted Johns and in honor of Paul Johns.

Celebrate life!

Steve

LEADERSHIP LESSONS

- **Connections = culture**
  Organizations and communities are held together by the connections between individuals. A key leadership goal should be nourishing and nurturing the multidimensional connections that define your culture. You can do this by supporting meaningful linkages that are both broad and deep, and by providing employees with options to connect and foster deep relationships with one another.

- **Community transcends function**
  A company culture can only truly flourish if the human connections on which it is based rise above the functional. Community matters and real community can only exist when people matter to each other.

- **Celebrate—don't wait**

  It is easy to get caught up in fast-moving events and the pressure to move onto the next goal . . . and the next. But if we don't take the time to celebrate what we have achieved, we squander a vital source of energy and motivation. More than that, we lose an opportunity to add meaning and happiness to our lives. So pause, evaluate, and celebrate before taking that next step forward.

CHAPTER 16

Be the Reason

Every day at OneCause, we are privileged to work with causes that are changing the world for the better. Our community of fearless fundraisers is an inspiring example of how individuals can make a real difference. They give us inspiring stories of life-changing teachers, ground-breaking research, animals and environments saved, and committed volunteers creating endless impact. Their work and that of the causes they support serve as a beacon for a better tomorrow. In a world that can sometimes seem dark, OneCausers are fortunate to be surrounded by our fearless fundraisers and their light.

We can all be catalysts for change. We all have the capacity to be the reason someone believes in goodness and hope. But tapping that capacity, putting that change into motion . . . well, it's not always easy. In fact, the task can sometimes seem so enormous that we despair at even beginning. That's why I'm grateful I never have to look far to find someone whose example challenges me to do more with my own life.

A recurring theme in my updates throughout 2020 and 2021 was the search for resources to help set ourselves in motion. With our workforce distributed to an extent we had never seen before, and traditional lines of management and oversight disrupted, every member of the OneCause Nation had to take on new responsibilities. We had to manage new workspaces, balance our home lives with work priorities, learn and share new virtual strategies with our nonprofit customers, and at the same time find the energy to motivate ourselves and push ahead to achieve new things.

I wanted to encourage every OneCauser at every level of the organization to think of themselves as a leader. We all have goals that only we know how to achieve. And we all have different sets of resources, drives, and motivations that we need to muster in pursuit of those goals. In a distributed world, leadership is democratized, and that can be empowering and scary at the same time. More than ever before, we need examples to inspire and encourage us to lead ourselves forward.

Throughout 2020, I often used the image of being in a fight against the virus, a battle that we could only win if we came together. In 2021, my thoughts turned more broadly to how we could apply a "warrior mindset" to leading and motivating ourselves. I loved how this framework for thinking about the world not only encapsulated our OneCause Values but picked them up from the page and gave them life in action.

The idealized warrior exemplifies curiosity, not simply standing steadfast in the face of the unknown but being excited by the possibilities that open up when we break the chains of the familiar. This mindset is shared by the explorer, keen to discover new lands, and the scientist who embraces uncertainty as the path to progress. That fearless outlook is what enables us to leave the certainties of today behind and build better tomorrows.

The Buddhist tradition gives us the example of another type of warrior who not only challenges themselves but also serves as an inspiration to others. In Buddhism, the central goal of every human life is "enlightenment"—leaving behind the pain and suffering of the material world to reach the peace and tranquility of Nirvana. But some of those who achieve this goal are said to give up the ultimate bliss that is their reward. Instead, driven by the pure power of compassion, they choose to return to the material world to help others work toward finding their own enlightenment.

The mindset of these saints, the "warrior bodhisattvas," provides an exemplary depiction of what it is like to be passionate, helpful, and committed. Like our fundraisers, we do what we do not just for ourselves but for the sake of others. We are committed to our customers, and we are passionate about helping their missions achieve everything possible. When we truly embrace these values, we have no choice but to lead the way forward, serving as examples for both ourselves and others.

We can't expect perfection. Try as we might, we are not always saints in everything we think and do. But we can choose the mindset through which we approach the world. If we choose to be warriors for ourselves and our causes, if we choose to fly our flag high and march forward fearlessly, we can make change happen. Even if we stumble from time to time, the choice to stand up and lead the way today has a transformative effect that can echo across a dozen tomorrows.

February 26, 2021

be the reason.

"Be the reason someone believes in the goodness of people."

—*Karen Salmansohn*

I heard this quote last week during "Random Acts of Kindness Week." It's the kind of quote that can stop you in your tracks. That's what it did to me.

I was in the middle of my morning mindfulness and stopped what I was doing for some self-reflection. Is that how people perceive me? Is that how I perceive myself?

Regrettably, my introspective answer was a disappointing "no, probably not." As much as I try to focus on the "why" of leading OneCause to our collective why of "Building Better Tomorrows," I'm pretty sure that "I'm not the reason someone would believe in the goodness of people."

BUT I can keep working toward that goal. It can be the "inspiration" that drives my "aspiration" to be a better person. To be aware of the opportunities in life to be kind, to go out of my way for others, to be generous.

We are so fortunate at OneCause. Every day we help those in need. Last week I tuned in to a Saturday night fundraiser for one of our customers—The Emerald School of Excellence (ESE) in Charlotte, NC.

What I discovered was unexpected. I have to admit that I did not know what cause the ESE championed. As I listened to a panel of young adults discussing their experiences, I learned that ESE was a "Recovery High School." Teens who have either dropped out or been asked to leave their high school seek to complete their academic pursuit while remaining sober and in recovery.

The way that they spoke about their executive director, Mary, brought to mind the quote. She is clearly someone who is **"the reason someone believes in the goodness of people."** These young adults finally had a place they felt welcome. Comfortable. At home. Among friends. Accepted. Understood. Loved.

You never know where you will find inspiration. But at OneCause you don't have to look too far. I found it on a Saturday night checking in on the performance of our new product.

I'm so grateful to be here with you beginning a new year, but also doing what we always do—helping make the world a better place—together with our nonprofit customers.

FEARLESS FUNDRAISING IN ACTION
Corey C. Griffin Charitable Foundation—Boston Winter Ball

In its 13th year, the annual black-tie Boston Winter Ball brought the fundraising to a more intimate, at-home setting featuring sponsored watch parties to support children and families through the pandemic. The organization created a variety of ticket packages for catered dinner parties, gourmet dining delivery, and at-home cook experiences in Boston and NYC.

The evening started with three Zoom room pre-parties with cocktail demonstrations followed by an at-home dining experience with a live entertainment from The Foodie Magician. The official program featured an awards presentation, silent auction, contests to win swag, raffles, and donation appeal.

Through ticket sales, sponsorships, and fundraising efforts, the evening raised astonishing funds—nearly matching their pre-pandemic raise during last year's event.

A final note to everyone who was impacted by the harsh winter weather from last week. Speaking as a lifelong Midwesterner, February is always a brutal month. We are so glad that you are now safe and warm.

We don't need a groundhog to tell us that March can bring some deadly winter weather as well. So, here's a quote to get you through the next "6 weeks of winter."

"In the midst of winter, I found there was, within me, an invincible summer."

—*Albert Camus*

Find your "invincible summer" within you.

Be the reason,

Steve

May 22, 2021

wake up.

Every morning last week, I woke up before my alarm. That doesn't happen that often.

Why? Why this week? Will it happen next week?

Wake up. Not just for yourself, but for the welfare of all beings. Wake up!

The Bodhisattva-warrior mentioned in this quote is a character from Tibetan Buddhist teachings. This warrior is brave and confident enough to overcome self-centeredness in order to help and serve others.

"Few of us are satisfied from retreating from the world and just working on ourselves. We want our training to manifest and be of benefit. The bodhisattva-warrior, therefore, makes a vow to wake up not just for himself but for the welfare of all beings."
Pema Chödrön

This is how I want you to feel about waking up every day—as a warrior for others.

- We're warriors for our customers and their causes.
- We're warriors for our family and friends.
- We're warriors for those in need—whom we don't even know.
- We're warriors for our colleagues, our teammates.

Our training, our expertise, our passion, and curiosity. Not just for our own benefit, but for the benefit of others.

So, what's been getting me up early this week? Anticipation. Excitement for our future.

Embrace of the unknown.

They were all calling to me—"wake up!"

"A warrior accepts that we can never know what will happen to us next."
Pema Chödrön

I want to wake up every day with the vow of the Bodhisattva Warrior—to wake up not just for myself but for the welfare of all beings.

As warriors, we embrace the unknown. We don't know what's going to happen next. We live in anticipation and rely on our training.

We've been jostled back and forth a lot over the past couple of months.

Virtual Fundraising Solution, please!

Wait! How about Peer-to-Peer for size?

And select all that apply:

- We're virtual.
- We're in-person.
- We're hybrid.
- We want services.
- No services please.
- No, make that mobile bidding.
- Product triumphs.
- Product setbacks.
- Customer delight.
- Customer stress.

I'm asked to forecast. You're asked to forecast. We don't know what's going to happen next.

But that doesn't mean that we should just throw our hands up. We need to *embrace the unknown*.

Next quarter? Second half? 2022? Four years??!! How about next week, Steve?!!

We need to be warriors and *embrace the unknown*.

Wake up each day for the welfare of all beings.

If we keep this mindset, we will grow. We will win. The answers will be revealed in time.

For today . . .

Wake up!

FEARLESS FUNDRAISING IN ACTION

The Indianapolis Colts Foundation—Kicking the Stigma

The Indianapolis Colts and the Irsay family launched Kicking the Stigma, an initiative to raise awareness about mental health disorders and remove the shame and stigma too often associated with these illnesses. In support of the Kicking the Stigma online auction, 495 supporters got behind this worthy mission.

The proceeds for the auction items, made up of meet-and-greets, autographed Colts memorabilia, and Kicking the Stigma swag, was 212% to value! In one week, the inaugural Kicking the Stigma awareness campaign had raised astounding funds which was then matched by Jim Irsay. The money will be used to support expanded programming for Indiana-based nonprofits working on mental health awareness.

QUOTE OF THE WEEK

"The most beneficial aspect of using OneCause is the support staff. Regardless of how simple a question or how difficult a question I had, their support staff always was patient and helpful and resolved my issues. [. . .] My event (the first virtual event for my school) went off without a hitch. I had total confidence that it would."

—G2 Crowd Review

As I'm writing to you, I'm on my way to the Bay Area to see my dad for the first time in a year and a half. He's 86 and in memory care.

COVID really set him back. Isolation. Loneliness. Lack of socialization. Lack of mental stimulation.

He's a warrior though. He wakes up every day not for himself. He wakes up with the goal of making someone else's day better.

Be a warrior.

Steve

July 16, 2021

no fear.

Does anyone remember that brand from the '90s/early '00s? This was my favorite hat back then.

I loved to wear it. I was in my 30's, I was kicking butt in the early days of PCs and the internet, and I was fearless.

It said something about how I felt and how I wanted to be perceived. That was then.

Life has a funny way of teaching us lessons. Life teaches us humility. Life teaches us about well, life.

2020 taught us a lot about humility. It also taught us to be resilient. We came back. Strong.

As we enter the second half of 2021, I'm going to put this hat on again—metaphorically of course—and I want you to wear it too!

Ask yourself this—if we survived 2020 and delivered the solid first half of 2021 that we did—what can possibly stop us?

What is it that we can't do?

> *"Give me a lever long enough and a fulcrum to place it on, and I shall move the world."*

> *—Archimedes*

Archimedes didn't even have our exec team, and he had the confidence to move the world!

We've got Stephanie, Tim, Karrie, Parrish, James, and Mark for goodness sakes!

And we have you!

That sounds like a *lever long enough* and the *fulcrum* to place it on. We can move the world!

no fear.

No fear doesn't mean no respect. No fear doesn't mean recklessness without planning or forethought.

But it does mean to embrace the unknown. Take on the tough challenges. Work together toward a common goal.

> *"The only way to make sense out of change is to plunge into it, move with it, and join the dance."*
>
> *—Alan Watts*

Even though we talk about going "back to the ballroom," we do so with great change.

Registration, check-in, check-out, entering your credit card, COVID safety protocols, greeting people, capacity constraints . . . change, change, change.

Change means something different to you depending on the mindset that you possess.

If you are fearful, change is threatening. If you are fearless, change is exciting. It is an opportunity.

> *"The only constant in life is change."*
>
> *—Heraclitus*

OK, so if we believe that the only constant in life is change, and we know that if we're fearful, change is threatening, we must be hopeful and fearless so that we see change as an opportunity.

no fear.

It's not just a slogan or a cool hat. It has to be our way of life. Change happens every day. We must greet it without fear.

Living our value of "We are helpful," then we must work with our customers to share the same mindset. No fear. #fearlessfundraisers

Let's put our "No Fear" hats on and go for it!

Who's with me?!

Steve

August 16, 2021

mindset.

I keep quotes and inspirational sayings in my Notes on my phone. There's one that I've been carrying around for a while now that needs to come out:

> *"It's not impossible. It just hasn't been done yet."*

I actually wasn't able to attribute that to anyone. There are a few modern-day leaders repeating it, but that doesn't count. I'm sure it predated George Blankenship and Tesla. ☺

I found another quote that has sparked some debate on social media over its attribution: *"The person who says it cannot be done should not interrupt the person doing it."*

That's great isn't it? There is really no better time for this way of thinking (and doing) than right now.

Mindset.

The sub four-minute (4:00) mile is a perfect story to demonstrate mindset. This mark stood for all of history and was generally considered to be humanly impossible.

Impossible that was until May 1954 when Roger Bannister ran the first sub-four-minute mile. What happened next? Six weeks later Bannister's mark fell, and then again and again.

In fact, there's a list online of 4,500 people who have officially broken the four-minute mile mark.

What changed? Mindset. The mindset of what was possible.

COVID keeps throwing us for loops, doesn't it? We were heading back to the ballroom with great strength and momentum and along comes the Delta variant, the return of mask-wearing, and the introduction of the "vaccinated vs the unvaccinated."

What's going to happen next? How many variants are we to face? Do we get to herd immunity? Are boosters necessary? What about kids now?

We've never experienced this before in the course of our lifetimes. **How do we know what is possible and what is impossible?**

Answer: We don't.

But we must approach these challenges with the correct mindset. The mindset that allows previously unachieved milestones to be broken.

The growth mindset vs. the fixed mindset:

Growth Mindset

- Views failure as an opportunity for growth and learning
- Embraces new challenges and explores the unknown
- Welcomes and embraces constructive feedback
- Focused on the journey over the end game
- Inspired and motivated by the success of others
- Pushes through obstacles to the finish line

Fixed Mindset

- Views failure as a limitation of abilities
- Avoids taking on new challenges or exploring the unknown
- Ignores and has difficulty accepting constructive feedback
- Focused primarily on looking smart and proving oneself
- Threatened or jealous by the success of others
- Gives up easily

I don't have the answers. Unfortunately, neither does anyone in seeming authority. So, let's:

1. View these challenges as opportunities.
2. Acknowledge and embrace our weaknesses and learn from them.
3. Be constructive.
4. Focus on the process, the journey.
5. Take inspiration from (and celebrate) the success of others.
6. See failure as a chance for learning.
7. Persist and grow in the face of setbacks.

I'm not even going to list the characteristics of a fixed mindset. Read them for yourself and then don't think about them again!!

We have to push the boundaries of conventional wisdom or limited thinking and imagine what **can be** and not just **what is**.

If we continue to do this for ourselves, our OneCause teammates, and our nonprofit customers, we will break through those barriers which are **seemingly impossible** to see beyond let alone break through.

You may remember—one of my first weekly updates was a list of things that I promised you we would do again someday. When I wrote it, the prospects seemed bleak, but we all knew intuitively we would do those things again.

Well, we're doing those things again.

If we all keep a growth mindset, we will win. Failure in that mode is literally **impossible**.

FEARLESS FUNDRAISING IN ACTION

Geauga Growth Partnership, LLC—Home Grown Geauga 2021

The Geauga Growth Partnership hosted its signature Home Grown Geauga fundraiser last Thursday to raise funds for their Youth Workforce Programs, which reach students in nearly every public, private, and parochial school in Geauga County, OH as they gain the skills they need to enter the workforce.

The sold-out event kicked off at the Sapphire Creek Winery & Gardens with a VIP wine and cheese reception before local chefs provided an amazing culinary experience for all attendees with a competition for the best dish. Geauga Growth Partnership went all out with the entertainment featuring multiple musical acts, living statues, tarot card readers, and a magician.

More than 300 in-person attendees and another 100 at-home supporters joined in the bidding in the silent and live auction, as well as purchased tickets in the cash and diamond raffles.

The evening concluded with a final "Call to the Heart" appeal that helped the 2021 Home Grown Geauga reach an impressive total raise.

With a growth mindset,

Steve

LEADERSHIP LESSONS

- **Change starts with belief**
  Every change starts with an individual believing that something new is possible. Real leadership inspires that sense of possibility at all levels of an organization.

- **Be a warrior**
  The ideal of the fearless but compassionate "warrior mindset" not only encourages everyone in an organization to believe that they can fight for a better future, it creates a resource to draw on in times of trouble.

- **No Fear: embrace the unknown**
  A positive approach transforms uncertainty from a threat to an opportunity. By embracing the unknown and moving forward to explore it together, we take on a tough but rewarding challenge. Not only can we shape the new world we set out to discover, the journey itself can help forge a common identity.

EPILOGUE

Gratitude

I've considered myself to be a "gratitude guy" since the early 90s. Growing up with a Lutheran pastor for a dad, giving thanks was a familiar business. Like everyone else, I also learned to say "Thank you" as a polite expression of gratitude in daily life. But these were almost automatic responses, rooted in the moment and pretty quickly forgotten. When I was introduced as an adult to the idea that gratitude could be a *choice*, an intentional decision to see the world in a positive way, that was something new to me. It felt like a tool for self-empowerment. I grabbed on to it and I haven't let go since.

Over the years, I've tried to make writing lists of things I am grateful for a regular part of my life. I always feel better when I do, and I always regret letting the practice go when I forget to do it for a while. But even when I let my gratitude journaling slip by, the idea is never far from my mind.

Gratitude has featured prominently in many of my updates throughout the pandemic. When we're faced with so many challenges and so much darkness, it seems natural to turn to a source of positivity and light that's available to us all. And there has been a lot to be grateful for, from the families and friends who have our backs, to the fearless fundraisers who journeyed with us and worked hard every day to sustain their own missions in the face of the pandemic.

But in two updates, gratitude wasn't just a supporting theme; it played the starring role. The motivation behind each update was very different, but that difference itself says a lot about the value of gratitude.

The first was written at the end of July 2020. We had just finished our first all-company get together since the start of the pandemic. Normally, this is something we do in person (see Chapter 15), but summer 2020 wasn't a normal time. We had passed through the initial wave of the virus and now numbers were starting to rise again. The four months we had been working from home felt like forever, but it was clear things weren't going back to normal any time soon.

In those months, we had all faced challenges and difficulties that were unparalleled in our careers. Despite the circumstances, OneCause didn't just endure. We pivoted our business and built a whole new platform.

We proved that distributed working was viable on a scale few of us had considered before.

And we stayed connected . . . to each other and our customers . . . in a way that made my heart swell with pride.

The opportunity to gather the whole team together and process those last months as a group was emotional for me. I was blown away by the sheer talent of the amazing people I had the honor of working with, and I was humbled by the reminder that they had stepped up to the plate again and again, despite the circumstances, to deliver the results our customers needed. When I began to write a few days later, the gratitude that had been bubbling up over the previous days came flowing out. It was something I felt incredibly deeply, and I wanted to share that.

My update in November 2021 drew from a different well. In the weeks leading up to it, I hadn't been feeling grateful for much at all. I was frustrated by the waves of new infections that we couldn't seem to get a handle on despite the success of the vaccine rollout. Putting our medium and long-term plans on the backburner each time the case counts ticked up was starting to chip away at my positivity. And the divisive bickering in the halls of power across the country wasn't making me feel much better. I wasn't feeling grateful. But that just made it all the more important to *practice* gratitude.

My frustration and anger were unreflective of responses to events going on in the world. Because I wasn't thinking things through and taking control of my responses, I was letting matters that were beyond my control dictate how I felt. In times like these, we need to sit down, take a breath, and remind ourselves of all the things we have to be grateful for.

If we *choose* to be grateful, we reframe the world and control our experience of it. Gratitude reminds us of what really matters, refocusing us on the things that have real meaning in our lives. By taking a moment to step out of the waterfall, to let go of the negativity, we reassert our power over the one part of the world that is truly ours to control: our mind.

Gratitude can be a blessing, a spontaneous response to events, and we should embrace it whenever we feel it. But it can also be a tool, a considered and thoughtful way of reminding ourselves what really matters to us. It doesn't have to be one or the other. I'm grateful it can be both.

July 24, 2020

gratitude.

I know it wasn't the same as being together, but I came away from this year's virtual company meeting with the same type of feeling that I usually do—man, do we have a great company! Thanks to everyone who came together to execute this awesome week!

Ted Waitt, the founder of Gateway and a very influential mentor of mine, used to say, *"A company is just a collection of awesome people rallying around a common goal."*

Ted was just a guy from Sioux City, IA who built Gateway from a two-person start-up in his family barn into a $9 billion publicly traded company. He saw the world so clearly.

That's precisely how I felt after this week. OneCause is a collection of amazing individuals working together toward a common goal and a shared vision.

And, how about those customer stories? Wow! I'm so grateful that I have the opportunity to serve this company and this community of fearless fundraisers! Talk about impact. Just wow!

The future is so bright!

We have the Vision. We have the Plan. We have the Team. We need to Execute.

So, thank you for taking a break from sawing that tree trunk to sharpen your saw. I know you are all incredibly busy trying to balance the demands of being a great spouse, parent, friend, and partner while also being the best OneCauser you can be.

At this halfway point in the year, I hope you were able to rejuvenate, remind yourself of the goal, and rededicate to finishing strong. I am so grateful for all of you. Thank you.

Since you got to see the full picture of Q2 and year-to-date results of all the departments, you're starting to see the context of how these weekly updates roll up into our continued progress.

Stay safe. Stay healthy. Keep on climbing.

Here's to finishing the 2nd half strong!

Steve

November 20, 2021

gratitude. revisited.

We always want more.

We're never satisfied.

I'm never satisfied.
That's what drives me (I think).
It provides fuel.
I think about what I don't have.
What's missing.
Rather than what I do have.
What I should be grateful for.

These updates have been no stranger to gratitude.
I've talked about it a lot with you.
But to be honest, lately I haven't been feeling very grateful.
I'm a little ticked off actually.
I'm frustrated that we can't get a handle on COVID.
I'm frustrated that case counts are going up again.
I'm frustrated that winter is coming.
And with it an expected increase in case counts.
That creates fear, uncertainty, and doubt (FUD).
Lack of certainty hurts our business.

Fear and doubt keep people in their homes.
I need a mindset change.
Happy Thanksgiving!
I'm grateful for Thanksgiving.
There's at least one day on our calendar to remind us to give thanks.

It's a day to pause and reflect.

It's a day to "give thanks."

It's a day for gratitude.

(. . . sound of needle scratching across vinyl record . . .)

What??!!

That's ridiculous.

Interrupt that pattern right now like scratching a needle across vinyl.

Your patterns are like the grooves in a record.

With repetition they get deeper and deeper-embedded.

Take a nail and run it across the grooves. It'll never play again.

I have to remind myself too.

That's what's great about these updates.

I'm writing to help you break your negative thought patterns.

To learn new techniques or manage through difficulties.

It also helps me.

New techniques serve as a reminder to me of what I believe and am committed to.

But what I may have forgotten about from time to time.

We all get caught up in the day to day.

We take the good things for granted and focus on the negative.

But here's the great thing.

Gratitude helps us establish protection from the inside.

Outside influences can't penetrate this inner resilience.

We all need reminders to break our negative patterns.

We need to make gratitude a regular part of our daily lives.

A habit.

Happy Thanksgiving!

Every day.

As I've documented over the years, we generally travel for Thanksgiving.

This year we are going "low-key" and have set up camp in Cocoa Beach, FL.

Home of Ron Jon Surf Shop and *"I Dream of Jeannie."*

I'm grateful for Cocoa Beach.

In 1972 my dad bought a little beach condo here.

He paid $12,000.

I was nine.

We spent many days surfing together in the blazing Florida sun.

Is it any wonder the only physical ailment my dad has is skin cancer??

Hint: Baby oil does not have SPF, Dad.

We still come here with my family.

I'm not nine anymore. ☺

It's become a place for contemplation and relaxation.

For family.
It is not fancy.
At all.
It's home away from home.
It grounds me.
It strips life down to the barest essentials.
There's no dishwasher.
It helps me think.
It gives me clarity.
I'm grateful for Cocoa Beach.

What's your Cocoa Beach?
Maybe it's a walk in the woods.
Skiing on fresh powder.
Your favorite chair.
A good book.
A fire in the fireplace.
Morning coffee on your back deck.
Taking a drive.
Playing catch.
Working out.
Running.
Watching your children sleep.
Spending time with a loved one.
Find it.
Then, take the time for gratitude.
Think about all the small things you take for granted.
Think about the big things too.
Write them down.

Review them with your morning routine and before you go to bed at night.

Studies have shown gratitude helps improve physical and mental health.

Lower stress hormones (cortisol) and higher joy (serotonin and dopamine).

What's your Cocoa Beach?

Write me a note back.

I'd love to hear from you.

Our world is crazy.

I'm still grateful.

Stop a moment and think about what we've been through.

We just set an all-time monthly record in October.

My first reaction?

"Why was it short of our plan?"

Come on, Steve!

How about expressing some gratitude?

I'm so grateful that our customers are getting back to fundraising!

I am grateful for all the donors and supporters who make things possible for our customers.

I'm so grateful for each and every one of you.

For those of you who've just joined us, I'm grateful for you.

You represent our future together.

That future is so bright.

There has been no better time to be at OneCause.

I'm grateful for today.

I'm grateful for you.

Happy Thanksgiving!

"Gratitude is not only the greatest of virtues,
but the parent of all others."

—Marcus Tullius Cicero

With gratitude,

Steve

Acknowledgments

I used to have a strong, disciplined gratitude practice. Every morning, I would journal my gratitude list, starting with my wife and family. The list was long. But I got out of practice. Maybe it was COVID. Maybe I allowed myself to get too busy. But there's always an opportunity to start again from where we are.

I'm reaching the end of this book, so I'll start again here.

I approach the expression of gratitude by starting with the image of a spiral or a series of concentric circles. I start in the middle and work my way out to the outer rings.

- The core of my gratitude begins with my wife, Sue. She knows me better than I know myself. She is my center.
- I'm grateful for my children Morgan and Griffin. They gave me my "why" before I found OneCause. They are my legacy.
- My dad is my hero and life inspiration.
- I've had my share of setbacks, but I'm grateful for my health—particularly as we have now witnessed COVID take more than a million lives in the US alone.
- I'm grateful for lifelong friends and mentors.
- I'm grateful for new friends with new perspectives.
- I'm so grateful for OneCause: my team, our customers, and the causes we all serve together. This collective is my new "why."
- And finally, I'm grateful for our country and the freedoms with which we are blessed. We're not perfect. We have a lot of work

to do. It's our great fortune to be blessed with the freedom to do that work.

Now, in theory you could continue this process almost indefinitely, moving further and further out to share your gratitude for the sun, the air we breathe, and even gravity itself.

As a practical matter, though, if you allow yourself a little time to hover over each item and pay attention to how it makes you feel, your heart will be completely full before you get even halfway down your list!

It's true. Try it!

With gratitude,

Steve

More from OneCause Nation

We were all feeling a general sense of fear, confusion and uncertainty. Steve's updates captured the emotions of the time in an authentic, clever and inspirational style that supported us through those challenging times. Steve's thoughts and perspectives on our shared experience provided a momentary sense of comfort that we were all in this together and his writing style with references to TV, movies, music, and philosophers would often bring a smile to my face and had me marveling at his creativity.

—Mark Ward (proudly, OneCause)

When the pandemic started, I was just happy to have a CEO who was really communicating. We were all worried about OneCause and about the nonprofits we worked with. What was really interesting was that somewhere around the third or fourth update, the tone shifted, and we got to see another side of Steve. He started sharing his reading, opening up his thoughts, and using the emails to share perspectives on life—his "silver linings of COVID." It made me feel more connected, and I was also like, "Yes! Someone gets what I feel, thank goodness!"

—Kelly Velasquez-Hague (proudly, OneCause)

One of the things that impressed me most was Steve's ability to keep up with the cadence. To put updates out every week seemed like a lot of work. So I really appreciated the effort that Steve was putting in. And then, as time went on, the emails started evolving, changing a little bit at a time and taking on this kind of inspirational messaging. But it wasn't corny. He was able to find something useful almost anywhere: TV shows, bands, philosophers. He was riffing off something new every time. And it really did help.

—Rick Seifert (proudly, OneCause)

The intention of doing them weekly during the pandemic showed everyone at OneCause that our leadership and company were determined, disciplined, and ready to take on the unknown with poise and perseverance. Through his lessons, learnings, challenges, and visions of hope, Steve led by example.

—Blair Carlin (proudly, OneCause)

Reading Steve's updates was like being showered with positivity. But it wasn't just a relentless and mindless positivity. He was honest about the stuff that wasn't working or about how he was hurting. And that sense of us all being in this together, it sort of made it feel like there was something positive even in the bad experiences, and if we looked hard enough, we could get something valuable from them.

—Joe Duca (proudly, OneCause)

The lockdown made me feel distanced from the company and my co-workers. Steve's weekly emails helped me feel connected and needed, like we all had a purpose.

—Mark Wilson (proudly, OneCause)

I'm always hungry for information, and with the pandemic upending everything, I wanted to know as much as I could about what was going on. But, especially at the start of things, it was hard to find anything that was reassuring or well-grounded. There was just a lot of baseless speculation flying around. Steve's updates were a great antidote to that. They were like an oasis of normality, stability, and reason. I came away from them feeling more informed, which was great, but I also came away feeling better about where we were and where we were going. And that was really important to me.

—Stephanie Ragozzino (proudly, OneCause)

I appreciated the perspective Steve provided in his weekly updates—it helped me to focus on the big picture and the good work we were doing in the midst of immense challenges.

—Melissa Donoghue (proudly, OneCause)

I don't remember ever feeling so lost as when the pandemic began. I had been with OneCause for over a decade. Seeing the whole fundraising sector under threat really struck my heart. But then Steve's updates started appearing in my inbox. His messages were so authentic, heartfelt, and inspiring that I found myself looking forward to them for a dose of strength and hope. He was looking out for us and our families, speaking to our hearts and reinforcing our values. He was taking care of us so that we could take care of the people who were strengthening our communities. They couldn't go dark; they had to keep going. And Steve was making sure we were all in a place where we could support them with everything we had.

—Dawn Lego (proudly, OneCause)

Steve got pretty personal in some of his updates. He was sharing details about his family, talking about what he was going through, and he was going through the same things as the rest of us. So it was nice to feel that we weren't alone. Even though we were all in our bubbles, there was a common experience that Steve was writing about, and it was something that linked us all together.

—Brad Ring (proudly, OneCause)

Steve truly brought all of us on a journey with him through the pandemic. His updates were his authentic self, they were helpful, relevant and really gave me hope. He inspired and connected with each of us in different ways. It was personally what I needed to hear so many times on any given week. I knew they were impacting others as well because they would come up in conversations. I am grateful for his passion and commitment to keep the updates going for so long, and even still today. He continued to shine a light for our future and really contributed to our success as a team.

—Karrie Wozniak (proudly, OneCause)

Reading Steve Johns' weekly updates made me connected and grounded, even amongst the chaos and unknown. Although I already knew that we were in good hands when the pandemic hit, hearing his thoughts each week reinforced that we would get through this together.

—Sarah Lewis (proudly, OneCause)

I think Steve started to express what we were all feeling. He was trying to connect with the entire organization to make us feel like we weren't alone. And we weren't! We had this Zoom family that started to form, where we were connecting with people on our computer screens. They were an outlet, a little window into the world outside my home. And Steve's updates put a framework around that, helping to create the feeling that these new ways of interacting were meaningful, that we were all part of something, that we weren't alone.

—Dan Gross (proudly, OneCause)

I started my journey at OneCause a few months before the COVID outbreak. I never predicted what was to follow and how my life would be impacted. As the world navigated the pandemic, OneCause and its customers navigated the future of fundraising and critical missions. Overnight, the entire company pivoted around fast-changing customer needs. It was incredible. I quickly appreciated that this was no ordinary company and Steve was not an ordinary leader. We were in it together, whatever it took. Steve's messages infused that attitude in all of us and his lessons on leadership in hard times are priceless.

—Tim Sublette (proudly, OneCause)

About the Author

Steve Johns is passionate about helping nonprofits build a better tomorrow. He leads the team at OneCause as Chief Executive Officer. Steve has more than 30 years of experience in technology, corporate development, venture capital, event production, and entrepreneurship. OneCause has emerged as the leading digital fundraising platform helping nonprofits raise more money and connect with their donors.

Steve brings a fresh perspective to his nonprofit tech role, blending his experiences in senior leadership at Fortune 500 companies with a successful record as an early-stage technology investor, scale-up business leader, and executive in the music industry.

He served on the Motorola Research Visionary Board, currently is a member of The Giving Institute, and sits on the Board of Directors for TechPoint helping guide growth initiatives for Indiana's tech ecosystem.

Steve is dedicated to building a people-first culture that balances individual well-being alongside collective business goals, seamlessly facilitating authentic connection, collaboration, and fostering inclusion and belonging for all. OneCause has been recognized with multiple 'best workplace' awards. He knows that for the teams at OneCause to serve their nonprofit customers, they must lead fearlessly together with a shared mission and purpose.

When he's not leading fearlessly, you can find him jamming to classic rock tunes in his office, walking the sands of Cocoa Beach with his family, or cheering on his beloved Chicago White Sox.

To learn more about Steve and his work at OneCause, connect with him on LinkedIn or visit fearlessfundraisers.com.